# A
# HISTORICAL
# ATLAS

1789-1971

for first examinations

*Second Edition*

R. R. Sellman

Edward Arnold

© R. R. Sellman 1971

First published 1963
by Edward Arnold (Publishers) Ltd.,
25 Hill Street,
London, W1X 8LL

Reprinted 1964, 1965, 1966
Second Edition 1971
Reprinted 1973

ISBN : 0 7131 1685 4

# FOREWORD

This Atlas is intended to cover the most popular 'A' and 'O' Level syllabuses of the English General Certificate of Education and the European or World History sections of comparable examinations elsewhere, and also where feasible to illustrate post-1945 developments. It includes maps from the author's earlier *Student's Atlas of Modern History* (Edward Arnold, 1952), and also a considerable number drawn specifically to illustrate fresh subjects or to give more adequate treatment to old ones. Social and economic diagrams have been added to provide some coverage for subjects less suitable for map treatment.

The Index is for location only, and each name has one reference: if the required information is not on the plate in question, it may be on another of the same area.

Relief and physical background have often been reluctantly omitted to allow clearer treatment of historical detail, and in such cases a geographical atlas should also be consulted.

R.R.S.

# FOREWORD TO THE SECOND EDITION

Within the same page-coverage, some maps have been improved and others have been replaced to give more satisfactory or more up-to-date treatment, while space has been found to include maps of Korea and Indochina.

As far as possible the original paging has been retained. Kilometre scales have been added, but not to the exclusion of miles.

R.R.S.

Printed in Great Britain by Unwin Brothers Limited, Old Woking, Surrey.

# CONTENTS

NORWAY
(Danish)
• BERGEN
CHRISTIANIA •
• STAVANGER

SWEDEN
GÄVLE •
STOCKHOLM •
GÖTEBORG •
KARLSKRONA •
ÖLAND
GOTLAND

FINLAND
(Swedish)
ÅBO • HELSINGFORS
ÅLAND IS.
(SW.)
VÄRÄLÄ
ANJALA
SVEABORG
VIBORG •
ST. PETERSBURG •
Ingria
NARVA
Estonia
DAGÖ
ÖSEL
Livonia
RUSSIA
RIGA •
Kurland POLOTSK •
MITAU • VITEBSK •
LIBAU •
KOVNO •
VILNA •
KÖNIGSBERG • MINSK •
GROSS
JÄGERNDORF •
BIALYSTOK •
Mazovia Podlesia
WARSAW •
BREST LITOVSK •
P O L A N D
Volhynia
KIEF •

DENMARK
AARHUS •
HELIGOLAND
(DANISH) •
COPENHAGEN
BORNHOLM
(DANISH)
Holstein
WISMAR (SW.)
HAMBURG • Sw. Pomerania
HANOVER
Mecklenburg
STETTIN •
BERLIN • P R U S S I A
DANZIG (POLISH) •
THORN •
POSEN •
KALISCH •
CRACOW •
Silesia
SAXONY
LEIPZIG • DRESDEN •
(Minor States)
HOLLAND
AUSTRIAN
NETHER-
LANDS
CALAIS •
LILLE •
MAASTRICHT
(DUTCH) •
LUXEMBURG •
Hesse
PARIS •
METZ •
STRASSBURG •
MÜLHAUSEN
(SW.) •
NEUCHATEL (PR.)
Baden
Würtemberg
BAVARIA
MUNICH •
HOLY ROMAN EMPIRE
Bohemia
PRAGUE •
Moravia
Galicia
LEMBERG •
Podolia
TARGOWITZ •
VIENNA •
PRESSBURG •
A U S T R I A
GRAN
BUDAPEST •
Bukovina
FRANCE
DIJON •
LYONS •
BERNE •
SWITZERLAND
Tyrol
TRENT •
GRAZ •
H U N G A R Y
Moldava
Transylvania
MOHACS •
TEMESVÁR •
Bessarabia
PIEDMONT
TURIN •
AVIGNON
(PAPAL)
TOULON •
PARMA
MODENA
NICE
GENOA
(REP.)
Venetian Rep.
VENICE •
FIUME •
Dalmatia
(VEN.)
Bosnia
BELGRADE •
Serbia
Wallachia
BUCHAREST •
KUTCHUK
KAINARJI
VARNA •
LUCCA • FLORENCE
SAN MARINO
(REP.)
Tuscany
ANCONA •
PAPAL
STATES
RAGUSA
(REP.)
Montenegro
SCUTARI •
NISH •
Bulgaria
T U R K E Y
Thrace
ADRIANOPLE •
CONSTANTINOPLE •
Corsica
(FR. 1768)
ELBA
ROME •
PONTECORVO
(PAPAL)
BENEVENTO
(PAPAL)
NAPLES •
MONASTIR •
SALONICA •
PHILIPPOPOLIS •
Sardinia
(Piedmont)
KINGDOM OF
NAPLES AND
SICILY
Ionian Islands (VEN.)
Morea
ATHENS •
PALERMO •
Sicily
MESSINA
CATANIA •
CERIGO
(VEN.)
CANDIA

CENTRAL
EUROPE
IN 1789

0   100   200   300   400 miles
0      200      400      600 km

TUNIS •

MALTA
(KNIGHTS OF ST. JOHN)

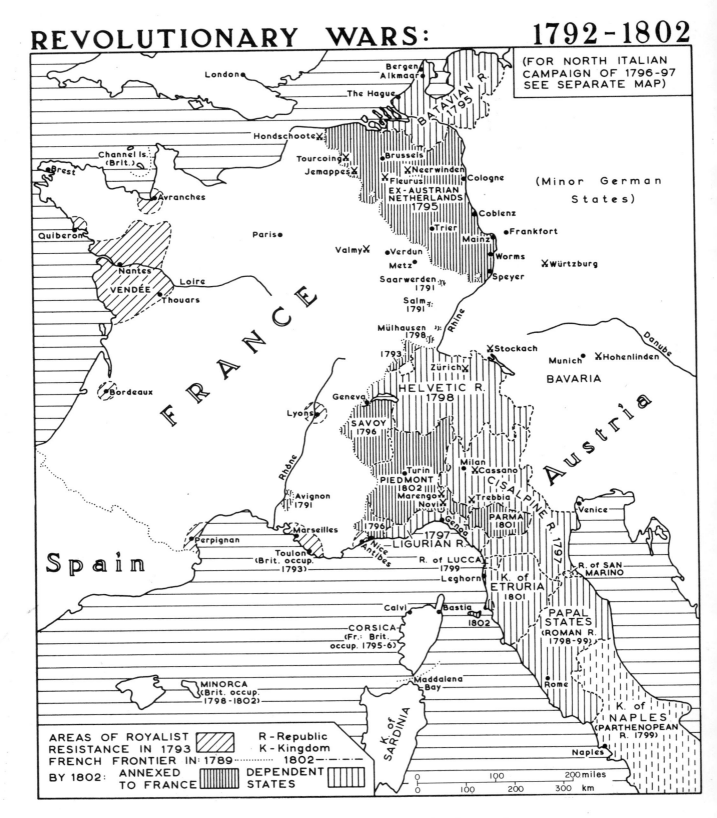

# REVOLUTIONARY WARS: 1792-1802

(FOR NORTH ITALIAN CAMPAIGN OF 1796-97 SEE SEPARATE MAP)

London

Bergen
Alkmaar

The Hague

BATAVIAN R. 1795

Channel Is. (Brit.)

Brest

Avranches

Hondschoote X

Tourcoing X
Jemappes X

Brussels
X Neerwinden
X Fleurus

Cologne

(Minor German States)

EX-AUSTRIAN NETHERLANDS 1795

Quiberon

Paris

Coblenz

Nantes

Loire

VENDÉE

Thouars

Valmy X

Verdun
Metz

Trier

Mainz
Worms
Speyer

Frankfort

X Würtzburg

Saarwerden 1791

Salm 1791

FRANCE

Mülhausen 1798

Rhine

Danube

1793

X Stockach

Munich

X Hohenlinden

Zürich X

BAVARIA

Bordeaux

Geneva

HELVETIC R. 1798

Lyons

SAVOY 1796

Avignon 1791

Rhône

Turin
PIEDMONT 1802
Marengo X
Novi X

Milan
X Cassano

C/SALPINE R. 1797

Austria

Perpignan

Marseilles

Toulon (Brit. occup. 1793)

Nice
Antibes

1796

Genoa

1797

LIGURIAN R.

R. of LUCCA 1799

PARMA 1801

Venice

X Trebbia

Spain

Leghorn

K. of ETRURIA 1801

R. of SAN MARINO

Calvi

Bastia
1802

CORSICA (Fr.: Brit. occup. 1795-6)

PAPAL STATES (ROMAN R. 1798-99)

Rome

MINORCA (Brit. occup. 1798-1802)

Maddalena Bay

K. of SARDINIA

K. of NAPLES (PARTHENOPEAN R. 1799)

Naples

AREAS OF ROYALIST RESISTANCE IN 1793
R - Republic
K - Kingdom

FRENCH FRONTIER IN: 1789 ⋯⋯ 1802 — — —

BY 1802: ANNEXED TO FRANCE    DEPENDENT STATES

| 0 | 100 | 200 miles |
| 0 | 100 | 200 | 300 km |

Piedmont was under French occupation from 1796.

6

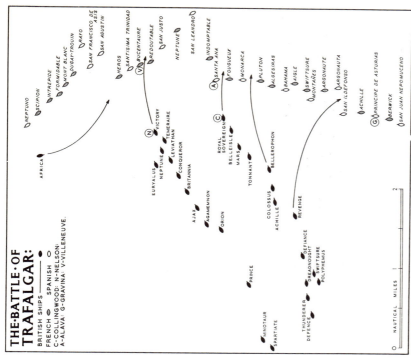

## THE·BATTLE·OF TRAFALGAR:

BRITISH SHIPS ◗
FRENCH ◖  SPANISH ◖
C-COLLINGWOOD: N-NELSON:
A-ALAVA: G-GRAVINA: V-VILLENEUVE.

French/Spanish ships (top): NEPTUNO, SCIPION, INTREPIDE, FORMIDABLE, MONT BLANC, DUGAY-TROUIN, SAN FRANCISCO DE ASIS, RAYO, SAN AGUSTIN, HEROS, SANTISSIMA TRINIDAD, (V)BUCENTAURE, REDOUTABLE, SAN JUSTO, NEPTUNE, SAN LEANDRO, (A)SANTA ANA, (C) INDOMPTABLE, FOUGUEUX, MONARCA, PLUTON, ALGESIRAS, BAHAMA, AIGLE, SWIFTSURE, MONTAÑES, ARGONAUTA, SAN ILDEFONSO, ACHILLE, (G)PRINCIPE DE ASTURIAS, BERWICK, SAN JUAN NEPOMUCENO

British ships: AFRICA, EURYALUS, (N) VICTORY, TEMERAIRE, NEPTUNE, LEVIATHAN, CONQUEROR, BRITANNIA, AJAX, AGAMEMNON, ORION, ROYAL SOVEREIGN, BELLEISLE, MARS, TONNANT, COLOSSUS, ACHILLE, BELLEROPHON, REVENGE, MINOTAUR, SPARTIATE, PRINCE, THUNDERER, DEFENCE, DREADNOUGHT, DEFIANCE, SWIFTSURE, POLYPHEMUS

NAUTICAL MILES
0   1   2

---

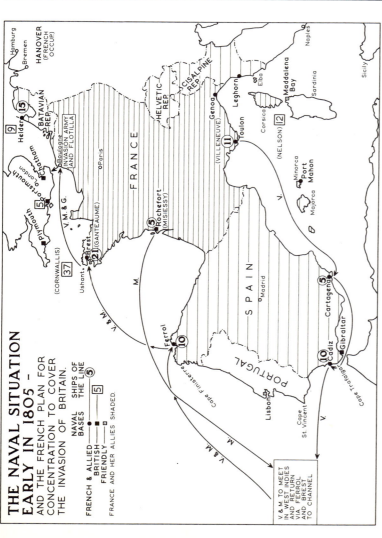

## THE NAVAL SITUATION EARLY IN 1805 -
### AND THE FRENCH PLAN FOR CONCENTRATION TO COVER THE INVASION OF BRITAIN.

FRENCH & ALLIED ●  NAVAL BASES ● BRITISH
BRITISH ■  SHIPS OF THE LINE 5
FRIENDLY □  □ 5

France and her allies shaded.

Hamburg, Bremen, HANOVER (FRENCH OCCUP.)
Helder [9], [15], BATAVIAN REP.
Chatham ■, London ○, Portsmouth ■, Plymouth ■ [5]
V.M. & G.
Boulogne ○ INVASION ARMY AND FLOTILLA
Paris ○
(CORNWALLIS) [37]
Ushant, Brest ■ [21] (GANTEAUME)
F R A N C E
Rochefort [5] (MISIESSY)
HELVETIC REP.
CISALPINE REP.
Genoa, Leghorn, Elba
Corsica, Sardinia
Toulon [11] (VILLENEUVE)
(NELSON) [2]
Minorca, Port Mahon, Majorca
Ferrol ■ [10]
Cape Finisterre
Madrid
S P A I N
P O R T U G A L
Lisbon
Cape St. Vincent
Cadiz [10]
Gibraltar
Cartagena [5]
Naples, Sicily
Maddalena Bay

V.&M. V.&M. M. V. V.&M. M.

V. & M. TO MEET IN WEST INDIES AND RETURN VIA FERROL AND BREST TO CHANNEL

---

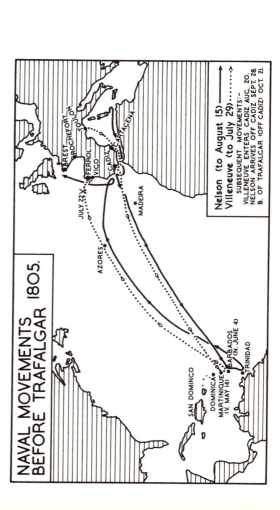

## NAVAL MOVEMENTS BEFORE TRAFALGAR 1805.

BREST, ROCHEFORT, TOULON, FERROL, VIGO, CADIZ, CARTAGENA
AZORES, MADEIRA
SAN DOMINGO, DOMINICA, MARTINIQUE (V. MAY 14), BARBADOS (N. JUNE 4), TRINIDAD
JULY 22 X

**Nelson (to August 15)** ──►
**Villeneuve (to July 29)** ·····
SUBSEQUENT MOVEMENTS:-  ─►
VILLENEUVE ENTERS CADIZ AUG. 20.
NELSON ARRIVES OFF CADIZ SEPT. 28.
B. OF TRAFALGAR (OFF CADIZ) OCT. 21.

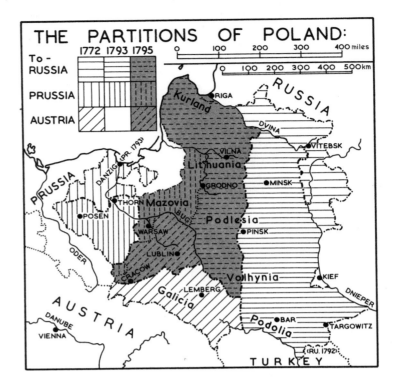

*First Partition*, 1772, arranged by Frederick of Prussia to compensate Austria for Russian gains in Turkey, while giving Russia territory with which Austria was not concerned.

*Second Partition*, 1793, results from Russian intervention to prevent Polish attempts to establish an effective government. Austria not involved.

*Third Partition*, 1795, follows suppression by Russia and Prussia of Polish national uprising under Kosciuszko: remainder of Poland absorbed by the three Powers.

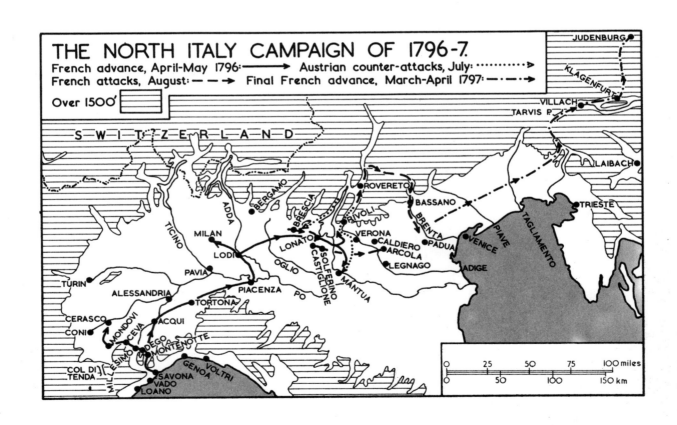

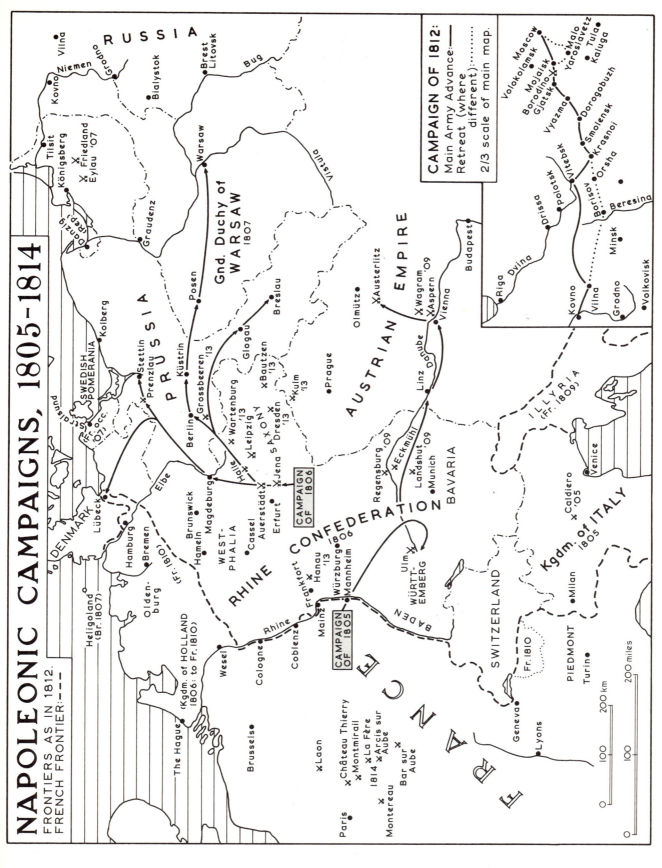

# NAPOLEONIC CAMPAIGNS, 1805–1814

FRONTIERS AS IN 1812.
FRENCH FRONTIER: ▬ ▬ ▬

**RUSSIA**

**PRUSSIA**

**Gnd. Duchy of WARSAW** 1807

**SWEDISH POMERANIA**

**DENMARK**

**WEST-PHALIA**

**RHINE CONFEDERATION**

**SAXONY**

**AUSTRIAN EMPIRE**

**BAVARIA**

**ILLYRIA** (Fr. 1809) A

**SWITZERLAND**

**Kgdm. of ITALY**

**FRANCE**

CAMPAIGN OF 1806
CAMPAIGN OF 1805

## CAMPAIGN OF 1812:

Main Army Advance: ▬▬▬
Retreat (where different): ·······
2/3 scale of main map.

Vilna, Kovno, Niemen, Grodno, Brest Litovsk, Bug, Bialystok, Tilsit, Königsberg, × Friedland '07, × Eylau '07, Danzig (Fr. Rep.), Graudenz, Warsaw, Posen, Kolberg, Stettin, Prenzlau, Küstrin, '13, × Wartenburg '13, Glogau, Breslau, × Bautzen '13, × Kulm '13, × Grossbeeren, Berlin, × Leipzig '13, Halle, × Dresden '13, × Jena × Auerstädt '13, Erfurt, Cassel, Magdeburg, Brunswick, Hameln, Lübeck, Hamburg, Bremen, Oldenburg, Heligoland (Br. 1807), Stralsund, (Fr. occ.), Olmütz, Prague, × Austerlitz '05, × Wagram '09, × Aspern '09, Vienna, Budapest, Linz, Danube, Regensburg '09, × Eckmühl '09, Landshut '09, Munich, Ulm ×, WÜRTT-EMBERG, BADEN, Würzburg 1806, Frankfort, × Hanau '13, Mannheim, Mainz, Coblenz, Cologne, Rhine, Wesel, The Hague, (Kgdm. of HOLLAND 1806: to Fr. 1810), Brussels, × Laon, × Château Thierry, × Montmirail, 1814, × La Fère, × Arcis sur Aube, × Bar sur Aube, × Montereau, Paris, Fr. 1810, Geneva, Lyons, PIEDMONT, Turin, Milan, × Caldiero '05, Venice, Elbe

100 200 km
100 200 miles

**CAMPAIGN OF 1812** (inset): Riga, Dvina, Drissa, Polotsk, Vitebsk, Beresina, Borisov, Orsha, Krasnoi, Smolensk, Dorogobuzh, Minsk, Volkovisk, Grodno, Vilna, Kovno, Volokolamsk, Moscow, Mojaisk, Borodino, Gjatsk, Vyazma, × Malo Yaroslavetz, Tula, Kaluga

The French occupied the Prussian fortresses of Küstrin, Stettin, and Glogau from 1807 to 1813: Swedish Pomerania was evacuated in 1810 but reoccupied in 1812.

9

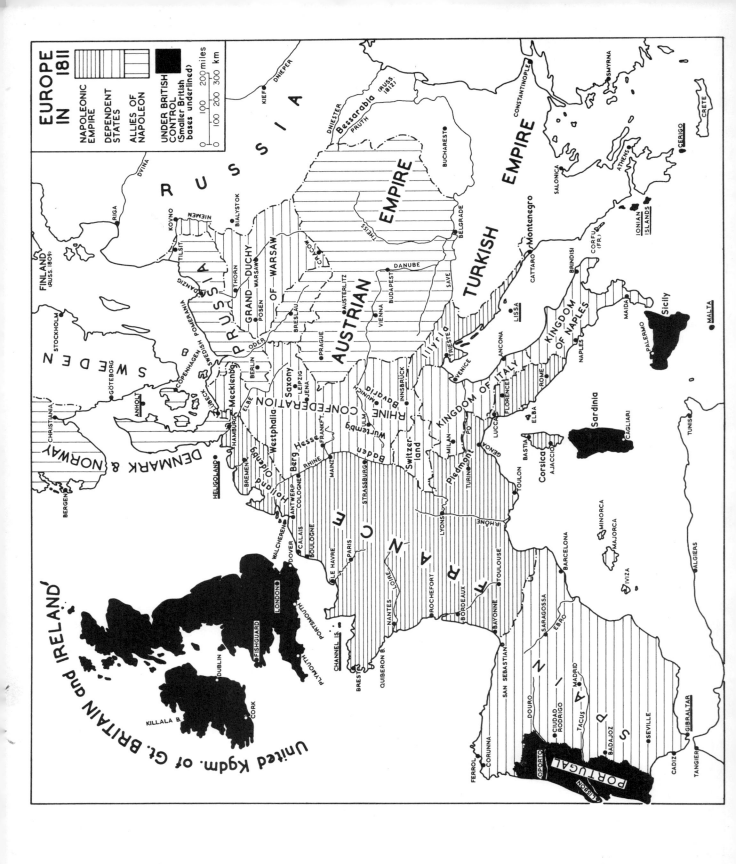

EUROPE IN 1811

NAPOLEONIC EMPIRE
DEPENDENT STATES
ALLIES OF NAPOLEON
UNDER BRITISH CONTROL (Smaller British bases underlined)

100    200 miles
100   200   300 km

RUSSIA

KIEF

DNIEPER
DNIESTER
Bessarabia (RUSS. 1812)
PRUTH

BUCHAREST

TURKISH EMPIRE

CONSTANTINOPLE

SMYRNA

CRETE

SALONICA
ATHENS
CERIGO

IONIAN ISLANDS

CORFU (FR.)

CATTARO
Montenegro
BRINDISI

LISSA
MAIDA

KINGDOM OF NAPLES
NAPLES

Sicily
PALERMO

MALTA

FINLAND (RUSS. 1809)

RIGA
DVINA

PRUSSIA

KOVNO
NIEMEN
BIALYSTOK
TILSIT
DANZIG
THORN
WARSAW
POSEN

GRAND-DUCHY OF WARSAW

MOSCA
THEISS

EMPIRE

AUSTERLITZ
VIENNA
BUDAPEST
DANUBE
SAVE
BELGRADE

AUSTRIAN

BRESLAU
ODER
PRAGUE

Illyrio
TRIESTE
VENICE
ANCONA

KINGDOM OF ITALY

ROME
FLORENCE
LUCCA
GENOA
MILAN
Piedmont
TURIN
PO

SWEDEN

STOCKHOLM
GÖTEBORG

NORWAY
CHRISTIANIA
BERGEN

SWEDISH POMERANIA
COPENHAGEN
LUBECK
Mecklenburg

DENMARK & NORWAY

ANHOLT
HELGOLAND

HAMBURG
ELBE
BERLIN
Saxony
LEIPZIG
JENA

RHINE CONFEDERATION

Westphalia
BREMEN
Oldenburg
Berg
Hesse
FRANKFT.
Wurtemberg
MUNICH
Baden
INNSBRÜCK
BAVARIA
ULM
Switzerland
STRASSBURG

Holland
ANTWERP
COLOGNE
RHINE
MAINZ

ELBA
BASTIA
Corsica
AJACCIO

Sardinia
CAGLIARI

TUNIS

UNITED KINGDOM OF GT. BRITAIN AND IRELAND

KILLALA B.
CORK
DUBLIN
PLYMOUTH
FISHGUARD
LONDON
PORTSMOUTH
WALCHEREN
DOVER
CALAIS
BOULOGNE

CHANNEL IS.
LE HAVRE
PARIS
BREST
QUIBERON B.
NANTES
LOIRE
ROCHEFORT
BORDEAUX
BAYONNE
TOULOUSE
LYONS
RHONE
TOULON

FRANCE

MINORCA
MAJORCA
IVIZA
BARCELONA
SARAGOSSA
EBRO

ALGIERS

SPAIN

SAN SEBASTIAN
MADRID
CIUDAD RODRIGO
TAGUS
BADAJOZ
SEVILLE
GIBRALTAR
CADIZ
TANGIER

FERROL
CORUNNA
DOURO

PORTUGAL
OPORTO
LISBON

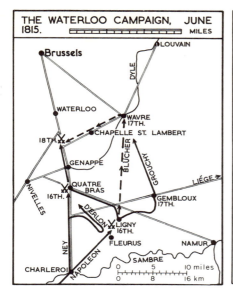

**THE WATERLOO CAMPAIGN, JUNE 1815.**

MILES

Brussels
LOUVAIN
DYLE
WATERLOO
WAVRE 17TH.
CHAPELLE ST. LAMBERT
18TH.
BLÜCHER
GENAPPE
NIVELLES
GROUCHY
LIÉGE
QUATRE BRAS 16TH.
GEMBLOUX 17TH.
D'ERLON
NEY
LIGNY 16TH.
FLEURUS
NAMUR
CHARLEROI
NAPOLEON
SAMBRE

0   5   10 miles
0   8   16 km

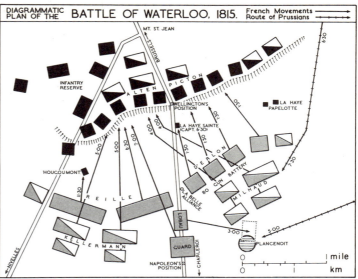

**DIAGRAMMATIC PLAN OF THE BATTLE OF WATERLOO, 1815.**

French Movements ———→
Route of Prussians ⊢—⊣—⊣

MT. ST. JEAN
BRUSSELS
INFANTRY RESERVE
ALTEN
PICTON
WELLINGTON'S POSITION
LA HAYE PAPELOTTE
LA HAYE SAINTE (CAPT. 6.30)
D'ERLON
HOUGOUMONT
REILLE
LA BELLE ALLIANCE
GUN BATTERY
MILHAUD
KELLERMANN
GUARD
NAPOLEON'S POSITION
PLANCENOIT
NIVELLES
CHARLEROI

0        1 mile
0        1 km

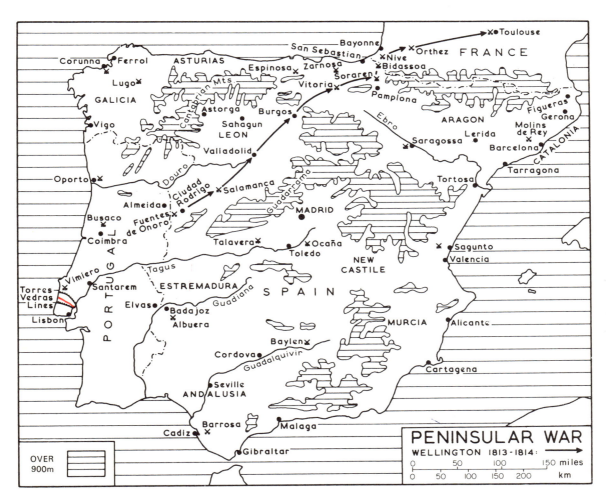

Corunna
Ferrol
ASTURIAS
Espinosa
San Sebastian
Bayonne
Zarnosa
Orthez
FRANCE
Toulouse
Lugo
GALICIA
Cantabrian Mts.
Vitoria
Soraren
Nive
Bidassoa
Pamplona
Astorga
Sahagun
Burgos
ARAGON
Figueras
Gerona
Vigo
LEON
Saragossa
Molins de Rey
Lerida
Barcelona
CATALONIA
Valladolid
Ebro
Oporto
Douro
Tortosa
Tarragona
Ciudad Rodrigo
Salamanca
Almeida
Guadarrama
MADRID
Fuentes de Onoro
Busaco
Talavera
Ocaña
Coimbra
Toledo
NEW CASTILE
Sagunto
Valencia
Vimiero
Tagus
Santarem
ESTREMADURA
S P A I N
Torres Vedras Lines
Elvas
Guadiana
MURCIA
Alicante
Lisbon
Badajoz
Albuera
P O R T U G A L
Baylen
Cordova
Guadalquivir
Cartagena
ANDALUSIA
Seville
Barrosa
Malaga
Cadiz
Gibraltar

**PENINSULAR WAR**

WELLINGTON 1813-1814

0      50      100      150 miles
0   50   100   150   200   km

OVER 900m

SWEDEN
AND
NORWAY

FINLAND
1809

BERGEN

CHRISTIANIA

HELSINGFORS
VIBORG
ST. PETERSBURG

Åland Is.

STOCKHOLM

REVAL
NOVGOROD

GÖTEBORG

RIGA
MITAU

DVINSK
SMOLENSK

DENMARK
COPENHAGEN
BORNHOLM
(DANISH)

KOVNO
KÖNIGSBERG
DANZIG
STETTIN
THORN

BIALYSTOK
BREST LITOVSK
WARSAW

KIEF

HELIGOLAND
(BRITISH)
Holstein
HAMBURG
BREMEN
HANOVER
BERLIN

P R U S S I A
POSEN
POLAND

Ukraine

Slesvig

AMSTERDAM
THE HAGUE
NETHERLANDS
BRUSSELS
COLOGNE
LUXEMBURG
FRANKFURT
MAINZ
GERMAN
(Minor States)
SAXONY
DRESDEN
PRAGUE
Bohemia
BRESLAU
Silesia
CRACOW (REP.)
LEMBERG
Galicia

P R U S S I A

FRANCE

PARIS
METZ
STRASSBURG
BADEN
Würtemberg
BAVARIA
CONFEDERATION

MUNICH

A U S T R I A

VIENNA
PRESSBURG

BUDAPEST

H U N G A R Y
Transylvania
HERMANNSTADT

JASSY

Bessarabia
1812
Moldavia

NEUCHATEL (PR.)
BERNE
INNSBRUCK
SWITZERLAND
GENEVA
LYONS
Savoy
Tyrol
Lombardy
PIEDMONT
MILAN
TURIN
Venetia
VENICE
TRIESTE
PARMA
MODENA
GENOA
LUCCA
MARSEILLES
MONACO (PRINCIPALITY)
NICE
TOULON

Dalmatia

Bosnia

BELGRADE
SERBIA
(AUTONOMOUS)
1817

Wallachia
BUCHAREST

SOFIA

ADRIANOPLE

CONSTANTINOPLE

Corsica
(Fr.)

SAN MARINO (REP.)
Tuscany
PAPAL
STATES
ROME
PONTECORVO
(PAPAL)
BENEVENTO
(PAPAL)
NAPLES

RACUSA
CATTARO
Montenegro

T U R K E Y

Macedonia
SALONICA

SMYRNA

Sardinia
(Piedmont)

KINGDOM OF
NAPLES AND
SICILY

Ionian Is.
(Brit.)

JANINA
Thessaly

ATHENS

Morea

PALERMO

Sicily

NAVARINO

TUNIS

Malta
(Brit.)

Crete

CENTRAL
EUROPE
IN 1815

0   100   200   300   400 miles
0      200      400      600 km

THE NETHERLANDS
1815 - 1839
FRONTIER IN 1815: ———
DIVISIONS IN 1839: ········
WALLOON AREA: ▦

0  10  20  30  40  50 miles
0              80 km

Ⓐ WALLOON LUXEMBURG EXCLUDED FROM
Ⓑ DUTCH LIMBURG INCLUDED IN
(GERMAN LUXEMBURG REMAINED IN THE
CONFEDERATION UNTIL ITS DISSOLUTION) GERMAN
CONFEDERATION
1839

(GRAND
DUCHY
1867)

The united Kingdom of 1815 ceased practically to exist with the Belgian Revolution of 1830 and Anglo-French intervention against the Dutch, but the Settlement was not completed until 1839.   The part of Luxemburg separated from Belgium in 1839 remained to the Dutch Crown until 1867, when, after the dissolution of the German Confederation (of which it had been a member), it became independent and neutral.

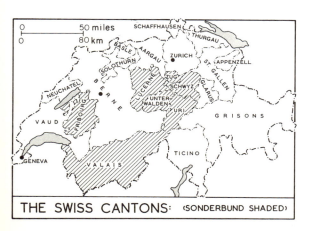

THE SWISS CANTONS:  (SONDERBUND SHADED)

THE EXPANSION OF RUSSIA IN
EUROPE:

B-BESSARABIA
K-KURLAND
E-ESTONIA
Z-ZAPOROCIA
I-INGRIA

ACQUISITIONS OF:-
ALEXIS AND
THEODORE, 1645-82.

ELIZABETH, 1741-62, &
CATHERINE, 1762-96.

PETER THE GREAT,
1689 - 1725.

ALEXANDER, 1801-25,
& NICHOLAS, 1825-55.

All other Cantons opposed the Sonderbund except Appenzell and Neuchâtel.   The latter became finally independent of the King of Prussia in 1857.

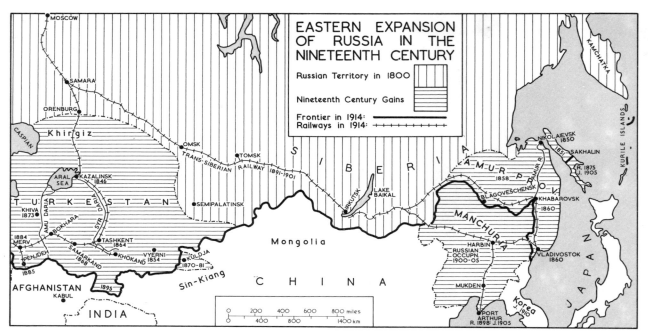

**EASTERN EXPANSION OF RUSSIA IN THE NINETEENTH CENTURY**

Russian Territory in 1800
Nineteenth Century Gains
Frontier in 1914:
Railways in 1914:

MOSCOW
SAMARA
ORENBURG
Khirgiz
CASPIAN
OMSK
TOMSK
TRANS-SIBERIAN RAILWAY 1891-1901
S I B E R I A
IRKUTSK
LAKE BAIKAL
KAMCHATKA
KURILE ISLANDS
NIKOLAIEVSK 1850
SAKHALIN 1851
R. 1875 J. 1905
A M U R PROV.
1858
BLAGOVESCHENSK
KHABAROVSK 1860
MANCHURIA
HARBIN
RUSSIAN OCCUPN. 1900-05
VLADIVOSTOK 1860
JAPAN
ARAL SEA
KAZALINSK 1846
T U R K E S T A N
KHIVA 1873
BOKHARA
AMU DARIA
SYR DARIA
SEMIPALATINSK
TASHKENT 1864
VYERNI 1854
KULDJA 1870-81
Mongolia
1884 MERV
PENJDEH 1885
SAMARKAND 1868
KHOKAND
AFGHANISTAN
KABUL
1895
Sin-Kiang
C H I N A
MUKDEN
KOREA
PORT ARTHUR R. 1898 J. 1905
INDIA

0  200  400  600  800 miles
0  400  800  1400 km

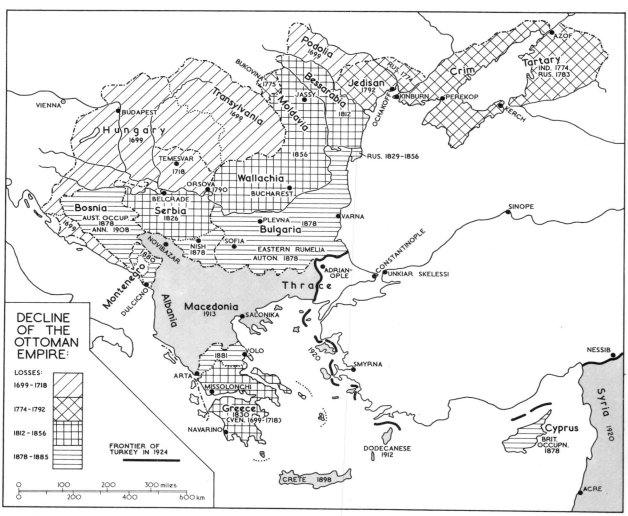

**DECLINE OF THE OTTOMAN EMPIRE**

LOSSES:
1699-1718
1774-1792
1812-1856
1878-1885
FRONTIER OF TURKEY IN 1924

0  100  200  300 miles
0  200  400  600 km

Podolia 1699
BUKOVINA 1775
Bessarabia
JASSY
Jedisan 1792
RUS. 1774
Crim
Tartary
IND. 1774
RUS. 1783
AZOF
VIENNA
Transylvania 1699
Moldavia
1812
OCHAKOFF
KINBURN
PEREKOP
KERCH
BUDAPEST
H u n g a r y 1699
TEMESVAR 1718
1856
RUS. 1829-1856
Wallachia
ORSOVA 1790
BUCHAREST
BELGRADE
Bosnia
AUST. OCCUP. 1878
ANN. 1908
1699
Serbia 1826
PLEVNA 1878
VARNA
SINOPE
SOFIA
B u l g a r i a
NISH 1878
EASTERN RUMELIA
AUTON. 1878
CONSTANTINOPLE
NOVIBAZAR 1880
Montenegro
DULCIGNO 1880
Albania
Macedonia 1913
SALONIKA
T h r a c e
ADRIAN-OPLE
UNKIAR SKELESSI
VOLO
1920
SMYRNA
NESSIB
ARTA
1881
MISSOLONCHI
Greece 1830 (VEN. 1699-1718)
NAVARINO
DODECANESE 1912
Syria 1920
Cyprus
BRIT. OCCUPN. 1878
CRETE 1898
ACRE

(For details of the changes of 1878–81 and 1912–13, see p. 24.)

THE GERMAN
CONFEDERATION
1815 - 1866

PRUSSIA   AUSTRIA

A —SAXE ALTENBURG
C —SAXE COBURG
F —FRANKFORT
G —SAXE GOTHA
GE—REUSS GERA
GR—REUSS GREIZ
H —HESSE HOMBURG
LD—LIPPE DETMOLD
M —SAXE MEININGEN
R —SCHWARZBURG RUDOLSTADT
SL—SCHAUMBURG LIPPE
SS—SCHWARZBURG SONDERSHAUSEN
W —SAXE WEIMAR

HELIGOLAND
(BRIT. 1807/14)

KIEL
HOLSTEIN
LÜBECK
OLD. M. ST.
MECKLENBURG
SCHWERIN
HAMBURG
LAUEN-
BURG
MECK.
ST. RELITZ
STETTIN

OLDEN-
BURG
BREMEN
ELBE

HANOVER
HANOVER
SL
LD
BRUNS-
WICK
ANHALT
MAGDEBURG
BERLIN
POTSDAM
P   R   U   S   S   I   A
DANZIG
KÖNIGSBERG
BROMBERG   THORN
POSEN

LIMBURG
INCL. 1839
P   R
WALDECK
SS
LEIPZIG
GLOGAU
LIEGNITZ
BRESLAU

AACHEN
COLOGNE
RHINE
HESSE
KASSEL
G W W
R A W
SS
GR
DRESDEN
SAXONY
REPUBLIC
OF CRACOW
AUST. 1846

TO BELGIUM
1839
NASSAU
DARM-
STADT
M
C
GE
F
INCL.
1818

LUXEMBURG
OLD. H
HESSE
PRAGUE
OLMÜTZ

BAVARIAN
PALATINATE
WÜRZBURG
NUREMBERG
PILSEN
BRÜNN

BADEN
STUTTGART
WÜRTTEM-
BERG
HOHEN
ZOLLERN
(PRUS.
1849)
ULM
BAVARIA
MUNICH
LINZ
DANUBE
VIENNA
PRESSBURG
BUDAPEST

LIECHTENSTEIN
INNSBRUCK
A   U   S   T   R   I   A
SALZBURG
KLAGENFURT
LAIBACH
SAVE

TRENT
TRIESTE

MILAN
VERONA
VENICE
PO
MANTUA

0   50  miles  100        150
0      80   km   160      240

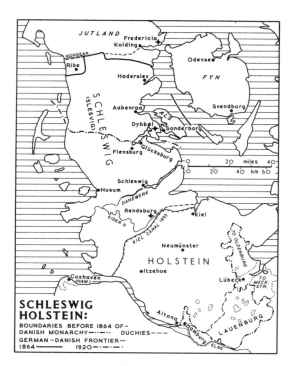

## SCHLESWIG HOLSTEIN:

BOUNDARIES BEFORE 1864 OF:
DANISH MONARCHY ———  DUCHIES ― ― ―
GERMAN–DANISH FRONTIER
—1864 ———  1920 ·—·—·

### THE WAR OF 1866.

Prussian & Italian
attacks on Austria →

Prussian campaign
against Confederacy →

Italo-Prussian
Alliance

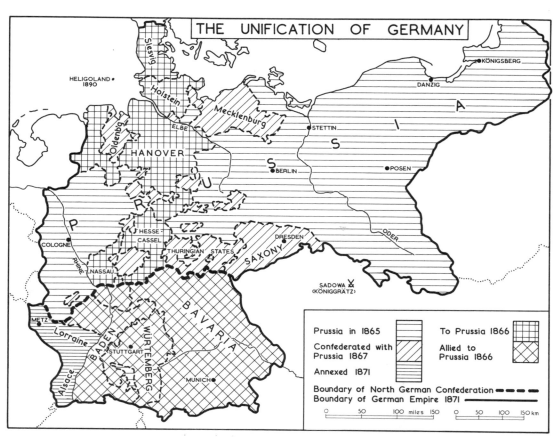

## THE UNIFICATION OF GERMANY

Prussia in 1865

Confederated with
Prussia 1867

Annexed 1871

To Prussia 1866

Allied to
Prussia 1866

Boundary of North German Confederation – – –
Boundary of German Empire 1871 ———

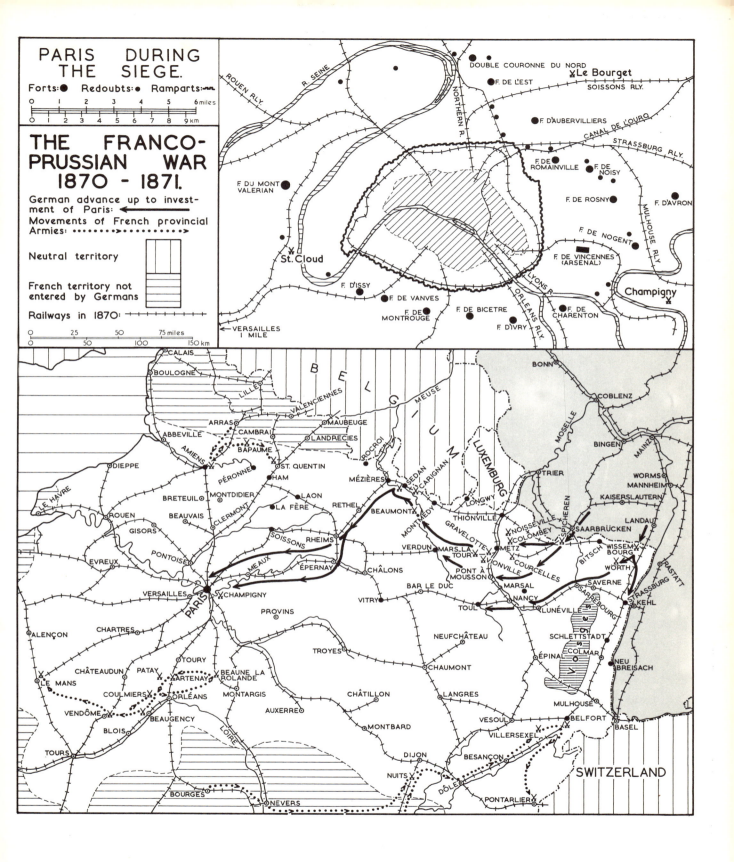

## PARIS DURING THE SIEGE.

Forts: ● Redoubts: • Ramparts: ⌁

0 1 2 3 4 5 6 miles
0 1 2 3 4 5 6 7 8 9 km

## THE FRANCO-PRUSSIAN WAR 1870 - 1871.

German advance up to investment of Paris: ←
Movements of French provincial Armies: ••••▶

Neutral territory

French territory not entered by Germans

Railways in 1870: ┼┼┼┼

0 25 50 75 miles
0 50 100 150 km

DOUBLE COURONNE DU NORD
R. SEINE
ROUEN RLY.
NORTHERN R.
F. DE L'EST
×Le Bourget
SOISSONS RLY.
F. D'AUBERVILLIERS
CANAL DE L'OURQ
STRASSBURG RLY.
F. DE ROMAINVILLE
F. DE NOISY
F. DU MONT VALERIAN
F. DE ROSNY
F. D'AVRON
MULHOUSE RLY.
F. DE NOGENT
×St. Cloud
F. DE VINCENNES (ARSENAL)
Champigny×
F. D'ISSY
LYONS R.
F. DE VANVES
ORLEANS RLY.
F. DE MONTROUGE
F. DE BICETRE
F. DE CHARENTON
← VERSAILLES 1 MILE
F. D'IVRY

CALAIS
BOULOGNE
BONN
B E L G I U M
LILLE
MEUSE
MOSELLE
COBLENZ
VALENCIENNES
LUXEMBURG
ARRAS
MAUBEUGE
ABBEVILLE
CAMBRAI
LANDRECIES
BINGEN
×BAPAUME
ROCROI
MAINZ
DIEPPE
PÉRONNE
ST. QUENTIN
MÉZIÈRES
SEDAN×
CARIGNAN
TRIER
WORMS
LE HAVRE
BRETEUIL
MONTDIDIER
HAM
LAON
RETHEL
BEAUMONT×
LONGWY
SPICHEREN
MANNHEIM
KAISERSLAUTERN
ROUEN
BEAUVAIS
CLERMONT
LA FÈRE
BEAUMONT×
MONTMÉDY
GRAVELOTTE×
×NOISSEVILLE
SAARBRÜCKEN
LANDAU
GISORS
SOISSONS
RHEIMS
VERDUN
THIONVILLE
×COLOMBEY
WISSEMBOURG
EVREUX
PONTOISE
MEAUX
ÉPERNAY
CHÂLONS
MARS LA TOUR
METZ×
COURCELLES
BITSCH
WÖRTH
RASTATT
VERSAILLES
PARIS
×CHAMPIGNY
PONT À MOUSSON
×VIONVILLE
SAVERNE
STRASSBURG RLY.
ALENÇON
CHARTRES
PROVINS
BAR LE DUC
MARSAL
SARREBOURG
KEHL
VITRY
TOUL
NANCY
LUNÉVILLE
TOURY
NEUFCHÂTEAU
SCHLETTSTADT
NEU BREISACH
CHÂTEAUDUN
PATAY
×ARTENAY
BEAUNE LA ROLANDE
TROYES
CHAUMONT
ÉPINAL
COLMAR
LE MANS
COULMIERS×
ORLÉANS
MONTARGIS
CHÂTILLON
LANGRES
VENDÔME×
BEAUGENCY
AUXERRE
MONTBARD
MULHOUSE
BLOIS
LOIRE
VESOUL
VILLERSEXEL×
BELFORT
BASEL
TOURS
MONTARD
DIJON
BESANÇON
SWITZERLAND
BOURGES
NUITS×
DÔLE
PONTARLIER×
NEVERS

17

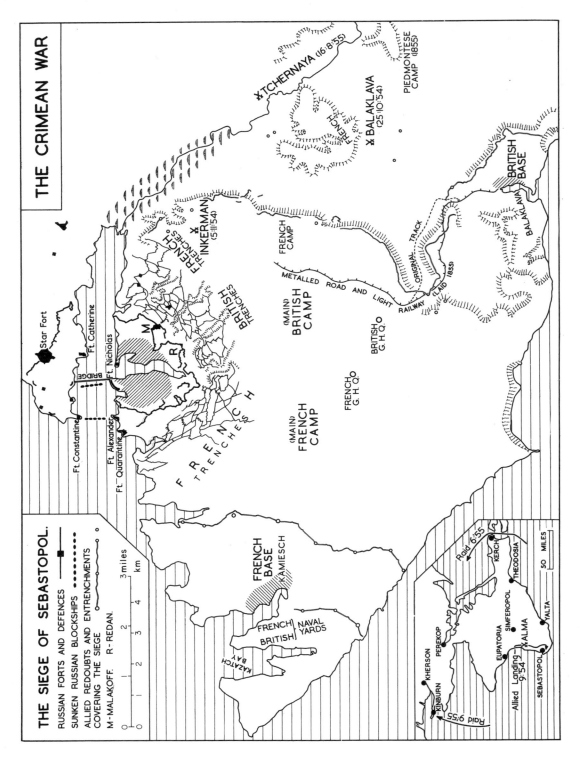

# THE CRIMEAN WAR

## THE SIEGE OF SEBASTOPOL.

RUSSIAN FORTS AND DEFENCES ▬▬▬
SUNKEN RUSSIAN BLOCKSHIPS ●●●●●●●
ALLIED REDOUBTS AND ENTRENCHMENTS ○○○○○
COVERING THE SIEGE
M - MALAKOFF.   R - REDAN.

0    1    2    3 miles
0    1    2    3    4    5 km

Star Fort

Ft. Catherine

Ft. Nicholas

BRIDGE

Ft. Constantine

Ft. Alexander

Ft. Quarantine

FRENCH TRENCHES

BRITISH TRENCHES

FRENCH TRENCHES

✗ INKERMAN (5:11:'54)

✗ TCHERNAYA (16:8:'55)

✗ BALAKLAVA (25:10:'54)

PIEDMONTESE CAMP (1855)

FRENCH CAMP

(MAIN) BRITISH CAMP

BRITISH G.H.Q.

FRENCH G.H.Q.

(MAIN) FRENCH CAMP

METALLED ROAD AND LIGHT RAILWAY (LAID 1855)

ORIGINAL TRACK

BALAKLAVA BRITISH BASE

FRENCH BASE

KAMIESCH

FRENCH NAVAL YARDS
BRITISH

KAZATCH BAY

Raid 6:'55

KERCH

THEODOSIA

SIMFEROPOL

EUPATORIA

ALMA

YALTA

SEBASTOPOL

Allied Landing 9:'54

PEREKOP

KHERSON

KINBURN

Raid 9:'55

50 MILES

Sebastopol was never invested on the north side, and had open communications throughout the siege.  The map shows the siege works as finally developed, when the French had taken over the right attack from the British, had captured the outlying Russian redoubts shown, and were about to make their successful assault on the Malakoff Redoubt.

**SWITZERLAND**

BRENNER P.
BOLSANO
TYROL
1919
TRENT

**1860**

1859
1866

**AUSTRIA**

SAVOY
(To France
1860)
ST. BERNARD P.
SIMPLON P.
ST. GOTTHARD P.

LOMBARDY
BERGAMO
BRESCIA
MAGENTA
MILAN
NOVARA
SOLFERINO
PALESTRA
CREMONA
TURIN
CASALE
MONTEBELLO
PAVIA
PIACENZA
ALESSANDRIA

VICENZA
PESCHIERA
VERONA
PADUA
CUSTOZZA
MINCIO
LEGNAGO
MANTUA

**VENETIA**
UDINE
VENICE

ISTRIA
1919
TRIESTE
FIUME
1924

MONT-
CENIS P.

PIEDMONT

**FRANCE**

PARMA
GUASTALLA
MODENA
PARMA

PO
FERRARA

**PARMA**
**MODENA**

BOLOGNA
Legations
Romagna
RAVENNA
FORLI

SPEZIA
MASSA & CARRARA
(TO MODENA 1829)
Lucca
(TO TUSCANY 1847)
LEGHORN
PISA
VOLTERRA
SIENA
FLORENCE
AREZZO

San Marino

ANCONA

MONACO (PRINCIPALITY)
NICE

**TUSCANY**

Marches
Umbria

CASTELFIDARDO

**TO PIEDMONT:**

By March 1860
By November

Route of Garibaldi's Force ——————
Route of Piedmontese Army ·············

Elba
ORBITELLO

**PAPAL**
**STATES**
TODI
TERNI
RIETI
Patrimony
CIVITA
VECCHIA
ROME
MENTANA

PESCARA
Abruzzi

Corsica
(French)

CAPRERA IS.

PONTECORVO
(PAPAL)
GAETA
TEANO
CAPUA
BENEVENTO
VOLTURNO (PAPAL)
NAPLES
SALERNO
EBOLI

**KINGDOM OF NAPLES AND**

Apulia
BRINDISI

**ITALY:**

**POLITICAL DIVISIONS**
**1815-1859**

0        50       100      150 miles
0   50   100  150  200    km

Sardinia

CAGLIARI

COSENZA

Calabria

**NORTHERN**
**ITALY**
**(PHYSICAL)**

OVER 1800m
OVER 350m

LIPARI IS.

MILAZZO
PALERMO
TRAPANI
CALATAFIMI
MARSALA

ASPROMONTE
REGGIO
MELITO
MESSINA
TAORMINA

CATANIA

**SICILY**

SYRACUSE

Lombard Plain
Apennines
Adriatic Sea

## THE AUSTRIAN EMPIRE 1815-1914

CARLSBAD
PILSEN
PRAGUE
ELBE
SADOWA 1866
CRACOW
VISTULA
PRZEMYSL
LEMBERG
TARNOPOL
Galicia
Bohemia
Moravia
OLMÜTZ
BRÜNN (BRNO)
Slovakia
MUNKACZ
Ruthenia
CZERNOWITZ
Bukovina
CARPATHIANS
LINZ
VIENNA
PRESSBURG (BRATISLAVA)
MISKOLCZ
SCHWECHAT 1848
Upper Austria
SALZBURG
Lower Austria
KOMORN
BUDAPEST
DEBRECZEN
GROSSWARDEIN
KLAUSENBURG (KOLOSVAR)
STUHLWEISSENBURG (SZEKESFEHERVAR)
INNSBRÜCK
Styria
GRAZ
H U N G A R Y
THEISS
Tyrol
Carinthia
KLAGENFURT
VILAGOS
SEGESVAR 1849 (SCHÄSSBURG)
ARAD
Transylvania
Carniola
PECS
SZEGED
SZÖREG 1849
TEMESVAR 1849
HERMANNSTADT
TRENT
GÖRZ (GORIZIA)
ZAGREB
MOHACS
DANUBE
Voyvodina
Banate of Temesvar
Lombardy
Venetia
TRIESTE
VERONA
Istria
Croatia
PETERWARDEIN
ORSOVA
BUCHAREST
MILAN
VENICE
FIUME
Slavonia
SAVE
BELGRADE
MANTUA
PO
POLA
Dalmatia
Bosnia
SARAJEVO
SANJAK OF NOVIBAZAR (MILITARY OCC. 1879-1908)
ZARA
MOSTAR
Herzegovina
SPALATO
CATTARO
SPIZZA (ANN. 1878)

Frontier of Austrian Empire in 1815: ———
Frontier in 1914 (where different): —·—·—
Boundary between Austria and Hungary: -------

Ceded 1859    Annexed 1846
Ceded 1866    Occupied 1878 Annexed 1908

0    50    100    150    200 miles
0  50 100 150 200 250 300 km

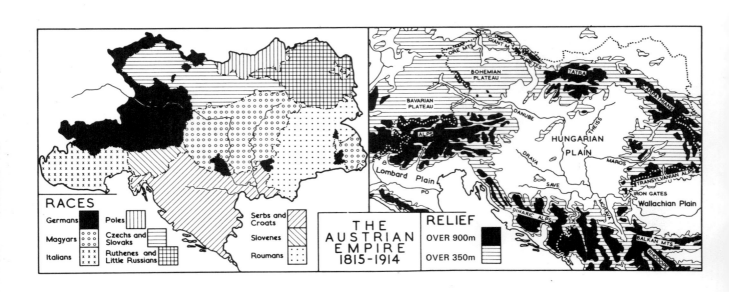

## RACES

Germans
Magyars
Italians
Poles
Czechs and Slovaks
Ruthenes and Little Russians
Serbs and Croats
Slovenes
Roumans

## THE AUSTRIAN EMPIRE 1815-1914

ORE MTS
GIANT MTS
SUDETES
BOHEMIAN PLATEAU
TATRA
CARPATHIANS
BAVARIAN PLATEAU
ALPS
DANUBE
HUNGARIAN PLAIN
THEISS
Lombard Plain
DRAVA
MAROS
PO
SAVE
TRANSYLVANIAN ALPS
IRON GATES
Wallachian Plain
DINARIC ALPS
BALKAN MTS

## RELIEF

OVER 900m
OVER 350m

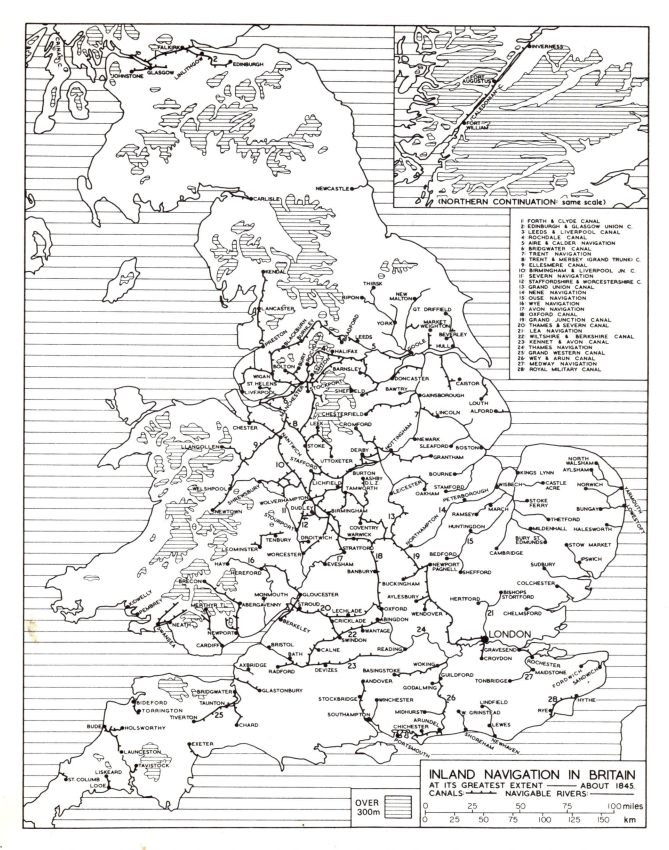

INLAND NAVIGATION IN BRITAIN
AT ITS GREATEST EXTENT ——— ABOUT 1845.
CANALS:——— NAVIGABLE RIVERS:———

OVER 300m

1: FORTH & CLYDE CANAL
2: EDINBURGH & GLASGOW UNION C.
3: LEEDS & LIVERPOOL CANAL
4: ROCHDALE CANAL
5: AIRE & CALDER NAVIGATION
6: BRIDGWATER CANAL
7: TRENT NAVIGATION
8: TRENT & MERSEY (GRAND TRUNK) C.
9: ELLESMERE CANAL
10: BIRMINGHAM & LIVERPOOL JN. C.
11: SEVERN NAVIGATION
12: STAFFORDSHIRE & WORCESTERSHIRE C.
13: GRAND UNION CANAL
14: NENE NAVIGATION
15: OUSE NAVIGATION
16: WYE NAVIGATION
17: AVON NAVIGATION
18: OXFORD CANAL
19: GRAND JUNCTION CANAL
20: THAMES & SEVERN CANAL
21: LEA NAVIGATION
22: WILTSHIRE & BERKSHIRE CANAL
23: KENNET & AVON CANAL
24: THAMES NAVIGATION
25: GRAND WESTERN CANAL
26: WEY & ARUN CANAL
27: MEDWAY NAVIGATION
28: ROYAL MILITARY CANAL

(NORTHERN CONTINUATION: same scale)

The Aberdeenshire Canal, running up the Dee valley from Aberdeen to Inverury, is not shown here.

21

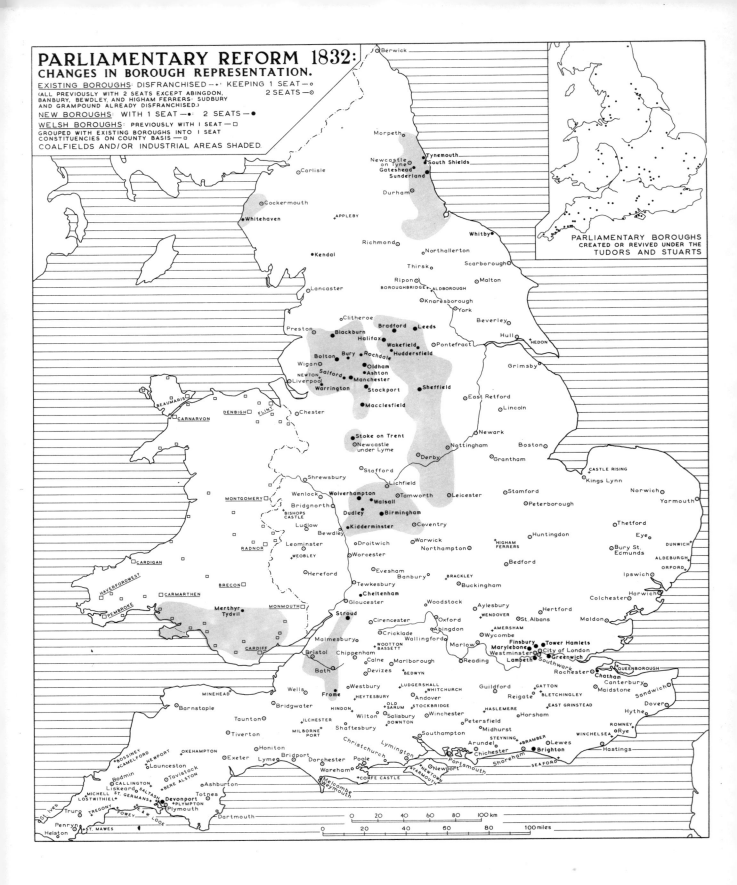

# PARLIAMENTARY REFORM 1832:
## CHANGES IN BOROUGH REPRESENTATION.

EXISTING BOROUGHS: DISFRANCHISED —•  KEEPING 1 SEAT —○
(ALL PREVIOUSLY WITH 2 SEATS EXCEPT ABINGDON,                2 SEATS —◎
BANBURY, BEWDLEY, AND HIGHAM FERRERS; SUDBURY
AND GRAMPOUND ALREADY DISFRANCHISED.)
NEW BOROUGHS: WITH 1 SEAT —•  2 SEATS —●
WELSH BOROUGHS: PREVIOUSLY WITH 1 SEAT —□
GROUPED WITH EXISTING BOROUGHS INTO 1 SEAT
CONSTITUENCIES ON COUNTY BASIS —□
COALFIELDS AND/OR INDUSTRIAL AREAS SHADED.

PARLIAMENTARY BOROUGHS
CREATED OR REVIVED UNDER THE
TUDORS AND STUARTS

Berwick
Morpeth
Newcastle on Tyne    Tynemouth
Gateshead    South Shields
Sunderland
Carlisle    Durham
Whitby
Cockermouth
Whitehaven    APPLEBY
Richmond    Northallerton
Kendal    Thirsk
Ripon    Scarborough
Lancaster    BOROUGHBRIDGE    ALDBOROUGH    Malton
Knaresborough
Clitheroe    York    Beverley
Preston    Bradford    Leeds    Hull
Blackburn    HEDON
Halifax    Wakefield
Bolton    Bury    Rochdale    Huddersfield    Pontefract
Wigan    Oldham    Grimsby
NEWTON    Salford    Ashton
Liverpool    Manchester    Sheffield
Warrington    Stockport    East Retford
Lincoln
Macclesfield    Newark
Chester    Boston
DENBIGH    FLINT    Stoke on Trent
BEAUMARIS    Newcastle    Nottingham    Grantham
CARNARVON    under Lyme
Derby
Shrewsbury    Stafford    CASTLE RISING
Lichfield    Kings Lynn
Wenlock    Wolverhampton    Tamworth    Leicester    Norwich
MONTGOMERY    Bridgnorth    Walsall    Stamford    Yarmouth
BISHOPS    Dudley    Birmingham    Peterborough
CASTLE    Thetford
Ludlow    Kidderminster    Coventry    Eye
Leominster    Droitwich    Warwick    HIGHAM    DUNWICH
RADNOR    WEOBLEY    Worcester    Northampton    FERRERS    Bury St.    ALDEBURGH
Edmunds    ORFORD
Hereford    Bedford    Ipswich
HAVERFORDWEST    Evesham    Banbury    BRACKLEY
CARDIGAN    Tewkesbury    Buckingham    Colchester    Harwich
BRECON    Cheltenham    Woodstock    Aylesbury    Hertford
MERTHYR    MONMOUTH    Gloucester    AMERSHAM    St. Albans    Maldon
PEMBROKE    Tydvil    Stroud    Oxford    WENDOVER
CARMARTHEN    Cirencester    Abingdon    Wycombe    Finsbury    Tower Hamlets
Malmesbury    Cricklade    Marlow    Marylebone    City of London
CARDIFF    Wallingford    Westminster    Greenwich
Bristol    Chippenham    WOOTTON    Reading    Lambeth    Southwark
Bath    Calne    BASSETT    Rochester    Chatham    QUEENBOROUGH
Devizes    Marlborough    Guildford    GATTON    Canterbury
Westbury    BEDWYN    Reigate    BLETCHINGLEY    Maidstone    Sandwich
Wells    LUDGERSHALL    WHITCHURCH    EAST GRINSTEAD
Frome    HEYTESBURY    Andover    HASLEMERE    Horsham    Hythe
MINEHEAD    OLD    Dover
HINDON    SARUM    STOCKBRIDGE    Petersfield    ROMNEY
Barnstaple    Bridgwater    Wilton    Winchester    Midhurst    WINCHELSEA
ILCHESTER    DOWNTON    STEYNING    Rye
Taunton    MILBORNE    Shaftesbury    Southampton    Arundel    BRAMBER    Lewes    Hastings
PORT    Salisbury    Chichester    Brighton
Tiverton    Christchurch    Lymington    Portsmouth    Shoreham
Honiton    Lyme    Bridport    Poole    NEWTOWN    SEAFORD
BOSSINEY    Exeter    Dorchester    Wareham    Newport
CAMELFORD    NEWPORT    OKEHAMPTON    Christchurch    YARMOUTH
Bodmin    Launceston    Melcombe    CORFE CASTLE
CALLINGTON    Tavistock    Weymouth
Liskeard    SALTASH    BERE ALSTON    Ashburton    Totnes
MICHELL    ST. GERMANS    Devonport
LOSTWITHIEL    Plympton    Dartmouth
Truro    Plymouth
TREGONY    FOWEY    S & W LOOE
St. IVES    Penryn    ST. MAWES
Helston

0    20    40    60    80    100 km
0    20    40    60    80    100 miles

22

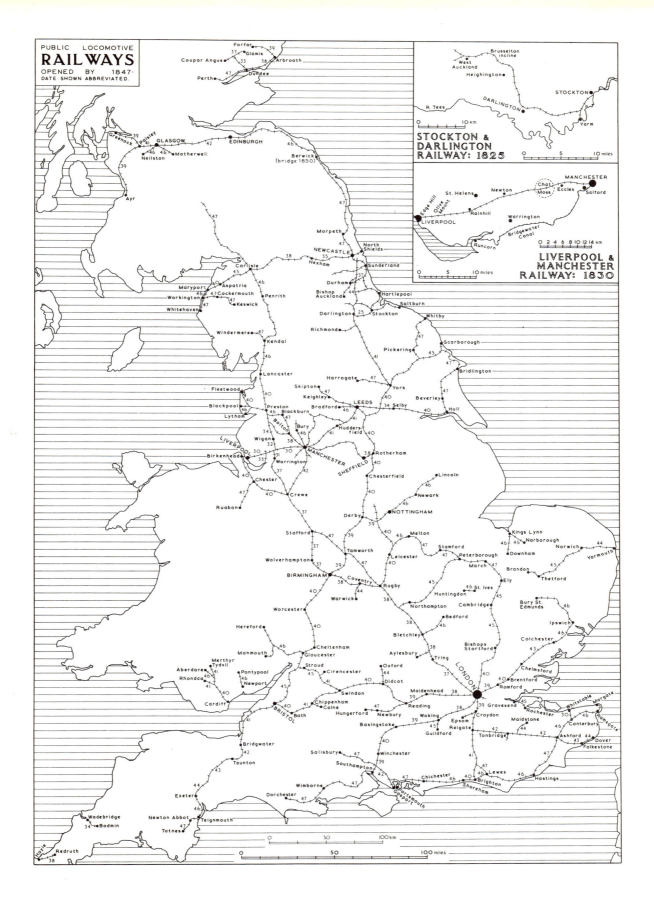

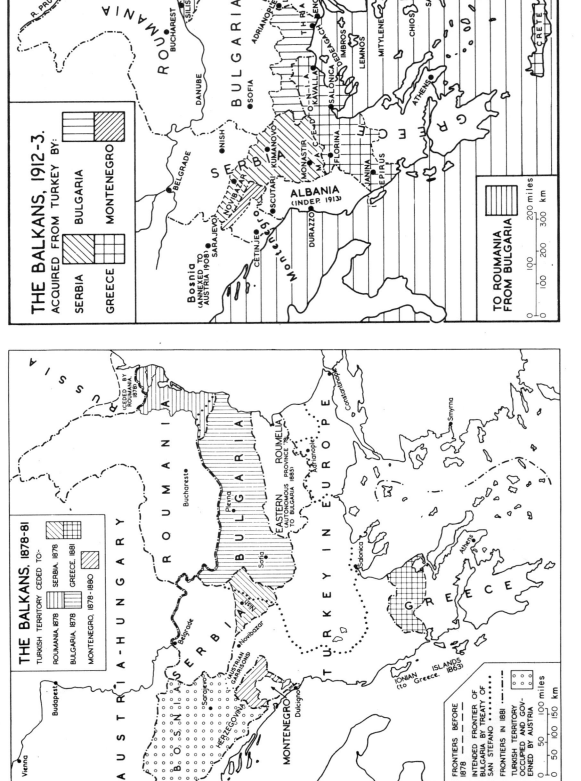

**THE BALKANS, 1912-3.**
ACQUIRED FROM TURKEY BY:

SERBIA    BULGARIA

GREECE    MONTENEGRO

TO ROUMANIA
FROM BULGARIA

R. PRUTH

ROUMANIA

DOBRUJA

SILISTRIA

VARNA

BUCHAREST

DANUBE

BULGARIA

SOFIA

ADRIANOPLE

KIRK KILISSE

MIDIA

LULE BURGAS

CHATALJA
LINES

CONSTANTINOPLE

ENOS

THRACE

DEDEAGACH

IMBROS

LEMNOS

SAMOS

DODECANESE
(ITAL. OCCUP.)

MITYLENE

CHIOS

BELGRADE

NISH

SERBIA

NOVIBAZAR

KUMANOVO

SCUTARI

MONASTIR

MACEDONIA

KAVALLA

SALONICA

FLORINA

JANINA

EPIRUS

GREECE

ATHENS

CRETE

Montenegro

Bosnia
(ANNEXED TO
AUSTRIA 1908)

SARAJEVO

CETINJE

DURAZZO

ALBANIA
(INDEP. 1913)

0   100   200 miles
0   100   200   300 km

**THE BALKANS, 1878-81**
TURKISH TERRITORY CEDED TO-

ROUMANIA, 1878    SERBIA, 1878

BULGARIA, 1878    GREECE, 1881

MONTENEGRO, 1878-1880

RUSSIA

CEDED BY
ROUMANIA,
1878

AUSTRIA-HUNGARY

ROUMANIA

Bucharest

BULGARIA

Plevna

Sofia

EASTERN
ROUMELIA
(AUTONOMOUS
PROVINCE '78;
TO BULGARIA
1885)

Adrianople

TURKEY IN EUROPE

Constantinople

Smyrna

Salonica

Athens

GREECE

IONIAN
ISLANDS
(to Greece, 1863)

SERBIA

Belgrade

NISH

Novibazar
(AUSTRIAN
GARRISONS)

MONTENEGRO

Dulcigno

BOSNIA

Sarajevo

HERZEGOVINA

Vienna

Budapest

FRONTIERS BEFORE
1878

INTENDED FRONTIER OF
BULGARIA BY TREATY OF
SAN STEFANO

FRONTIERS IN 1881

TURKISH TERRITORY
OCCUPIED AND GOV-
ERNED BY AUSTRIA

0   50   100 miles
0   50   100   150 km

All the Aegean islands except Imbros (and the Dodecanese, already occupied by Italy) fell into Greek hands during the First Balkan War, but were not formally ceded until 1920.

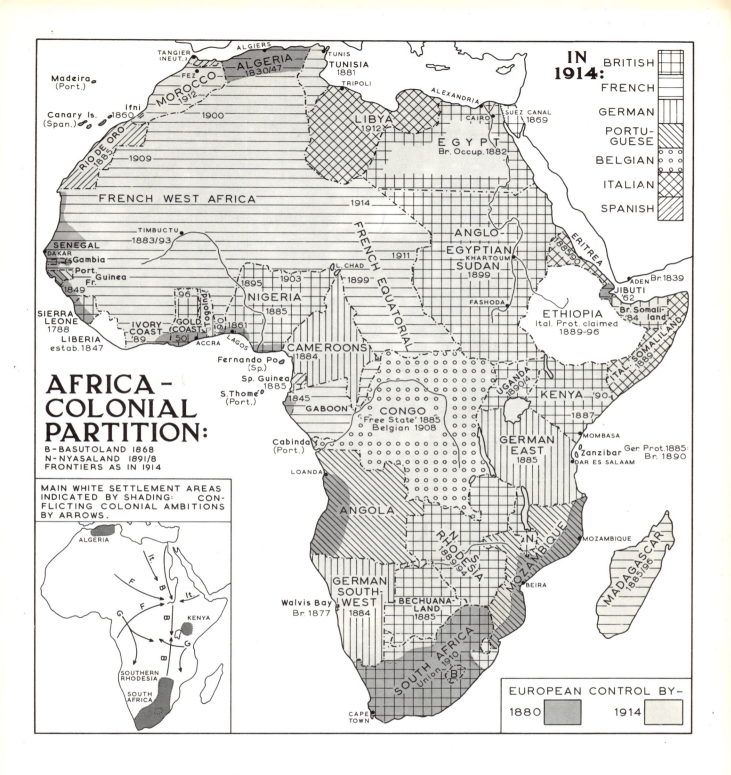

IN 1914:

- BRITISH
- FRENCH
- GERMAN
- PORTU-GUESE
- BELGIAN
- ITALIAN
- SPANISH

Madeira (Port.)

Canary Is. (Span.)

TANGIER (NEUT.)
ALGIERS
TUNIS
ALGERIA 1830/47
TUNISIA 1881
FEZ
MOROCCO 1912
Ifni 1860
1900
RIO DE ORO 1885
1909

TRIPOLI
LIBYA 1912
ALEXANDRIA
CAIRO
SUEZ CANAL 1869
EGYPT Br. Occup. 1882

FRENCH WEST AFRICA
1914

TIMBUCTU 1883/93
1911
ANGLO-EGYPTIAN SUDAN KHARTOUM 1899
ERITREA 1885/90
ADEN Br. 1839
JIBUTI '62
Br. Somali-land '84

SENEGAL
DAKAR
Gambia Port.
Fr. Guinea
1849
1895  1903
NIGERIA 1885
L. CHAD
1899
FASHODA
ETHIOPIA Ital. Prot. claimed 1889-96
ITAL. SOMALILAND 1889

SIERRA LEONE 1788
LIBERIA estab. 1847
IVORY COAST '89
GOLD COAST '50
1861
ACCRA
LAGOS
CAMEROONS 1884
Fernando Po (Sp.)
Sp. Guinea 1885
S. Thomé (Port.)
1845
GABOON

FRENCH EQUATORIAL

UGANDA 1890/4
KENYA '90
1887
MOMBASA
GERMAN EAST 1885
Zanzibar
DAR ES SALAAM
Ger. Prot. 1885 Br. 1890

AFRICA – COLONIAL PARTITION:

B–BASUTOLAND 1868
N–NYASALAND 1891/8
FRONTIERS AS IN 1914

Cabinda (Port.)
CONGO 'Free State' 1885 Belgian 1908
LOANDA

MAIN WHITE SETTLEMENT AREAS INDICATED BY SHADING: CONFLICTING COLONIAL AMBITIONS BY ARROWS.

ALGERIA

It.
F
F
G
B
It.
B
KENYA
G
B
B
SOUTHERN RHODESIA
SOUTH AFRICA

ANGOLA
RHODESIA 1889/4
N. MOZAMBIQUE
MOZAMBIQUE
MADAGASCAR 1885/96
BEIRA

Walvis Bay Br. 1877
GERMAN SOUTH-WEST 1884
BECHUANA-LAND 1885
SOUTH AFRICA Union 1910
B
CAPE TOWN

EUROPEAN CONTROL BY–
1880    1914

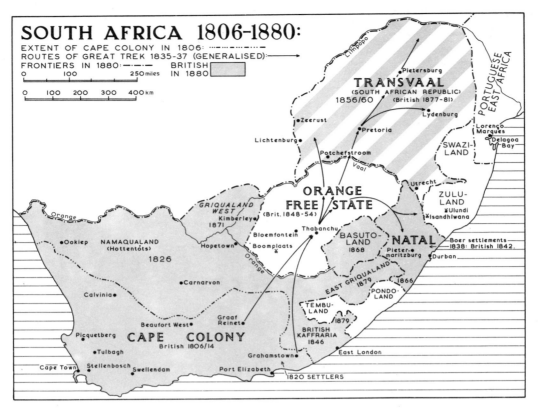

## SOUTH AFRICA 1806-1880:

EXTENT OF CAPE COLONY IN 1806: ·········
ROUTES OF GREAT TREK 1835-37 (GENERALISED): ⟶
FRONTIERS IN 1880: —·—·—    BRITISH IN 1880: ▨

0      100                  250 miles
0   100   200   300   400 km

**TRANSVAAL**
1856/60 (SOUTH AFRICAN REPUBLIC) (British 1877-81)

PORTUGUESE EAST AFRICA

Limpopo
•Pietersburg
•Zeerust
Lichtenburg•        •Pretoria        •Lydenburg
                                              Lorenço
                                              Marques
                    •Potchefstroom                •Delagoa
                              Vaal                  Bay
                                      SWAZI-
                                      LAND

**ORANGE FREE STATE**        •Utrecht
(Brit.1848-54)                        ZULU-
GRIQUALAND                             LAND
WEST                                  ⚔Ulundi
Kimberley•                             ⚔Isandhlwana
1871                 BASUTO-
•Ookiep  NAMAQUALAND    Bloemfontein•  LAND    **NATAL**
         (Hottentots)  Boomplaats×  1868   Pieter-  Boer settlements
                       Thabanchu×        maritzburg• 1838: British 1842.
Hopetown•                          •        •Durban
          1826            Orange
                                   EAST GRIQUALAND
         •Carnarvon                1879    1866
                                   PONDO-
Calvinia•                          TEMBU-  LAND
                                   LAND
         Beaufort West• •Graaf    1879
                        Reinet    BRITISH
Picquetberg•   **CAPE COLONY**    KAFFRARIA
                British 1806/14   1846
•Tulbagh                          East London
Cape Town•  Stellenbosch•  •Grahamstown
        •Swellendam   Port Elizabeth•
                      1820 SETTLERS

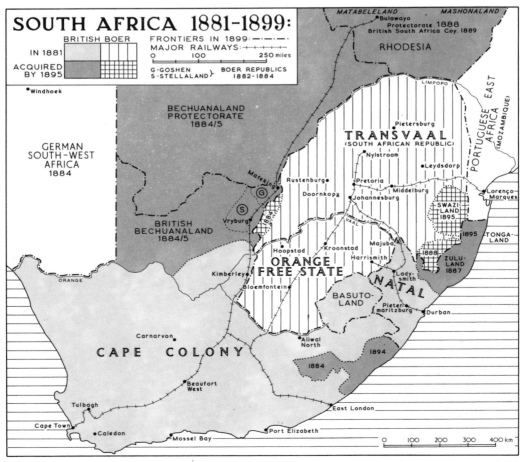

## SOUTH AFRICA 1881-1899:

            BRITISH  BOER
IN 1881      ▨      ▦
ACQUIRED    ▦      ▦
BY 1895

FRONTIERS IN 1899: —·—·—
MAJOR RAILWAYS: ┼┼┼┼┼
0        100              250 miles
G-GOSHEN           BOER REPUBLICS
S-STELLALAND       1882-1884

MATABELELAND          MASHONALAND
        •Bulawayo
        Protectorate 1888
        British South Africa Coy. 1889
                RHODESIA

•Windhoek
                BECHUANALAND
                PROTECTORATE
                1884/5
GERMAN                              Limpopo       PORTUGUESE EAST
SOUTH-WEST                                        AFRICA (MOZAMBIQUE)
AFRICA                          **TRANSVAAL**
1884                            (SOUTH AFRICAN REPUBLIC)
                                •Pietersburg
                    Mafeking    •Nylstroom
                    ⓖ  •Rustenburg  •Leydsdorp
        BRITISH     ⓢ  Doornkop× •Pretoria  Lorenço
        BECHUANALAND Vryburg•  •Johannesburg  •Middelburg  Marques
        1884/5                              SWAZI-  TONGA-
                    1884      Vaal          LAND   LAND
                    •Hoopstad  •Kroonstad    1895   1895
ORANGE            Kimberley• **FREE STATE**  Majuba  ⊞1888  ZULU-
                          Harrismith         1888    LAND
         •Bloemfontein                Lady-          1887
                                      smith
         **CAPE COLONY**        BASUTO-  **NATAL**
•Carnarvon                      LAND   Pieter-
                                       maritzburg•  •Durban
                    Aliwal
                    North    1894
                  1884
        •Beaufort
         West
                            East London
•Tulbagh
Cape Town•  •Caledon
        •Mossel Bay   Port Elizabeth•
                      0  100  200  300  400 km

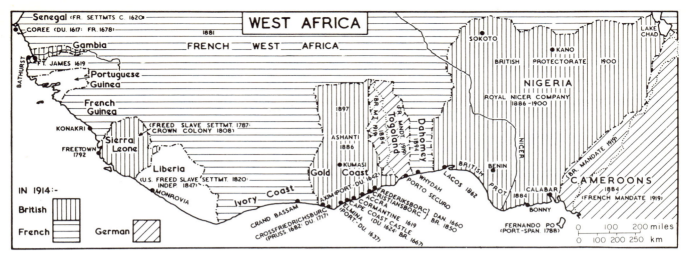

# WEST AFRICA

Senegal (FR. SETTMTS C. 1620)
COREE (DU. 1617; FR. 1678)
1881
FRENCH WEST AFRICA
BATHURST
Gambia
FT. JAMES 1619
Portuguese Guinea
French Guinea
KONAKRI
(FREED SLAVE SETTMT. 1787;
CROWN COLONY 1808)
1897
SOKOTO
KANO
BRITISH PROTECTORATE 1900
NIGERIA
ROYAL NIGER COMPANY 1886-1900
LAKE CHAD
Sierra Leone
FREETOWN 1792
Liberia
(U.S. FREED SLAVE SETTMT. 1820.
INDEP. 1847)
MONROVIA
Ivory Coast
GRAND BASSAM
CROSSFRIEDRICHSBURG
(PRUSS. 1682; DU. 1717)
ASHANTI 1886
KUMASI
Gold Coast
AXIM (PORT. DU. 1642)
ELMINA (PORT. DU. 1637)
CAPE COAST CASTLE (DU. 1624; BR. 1667)
CORMANTINE 1619
ACCRA (ANSBORG)
FREDERIKSBORG
Togoland
Dahomey 1894
PORTO SEGURO
WHYDAH
DAN. 1660
LACOS 1862
BENIN
BONNY
CALABAR 1884
FERNANDO PO (PORT.-SPAN. 1788)
BR. PROT.
NICER
CAMEROONS 1884
(FRENCH MANDATE 1919)
BR. MANDATE 1919

IN 1914:-
British
French
German

0   100   200 miles
0   100 200 250 km

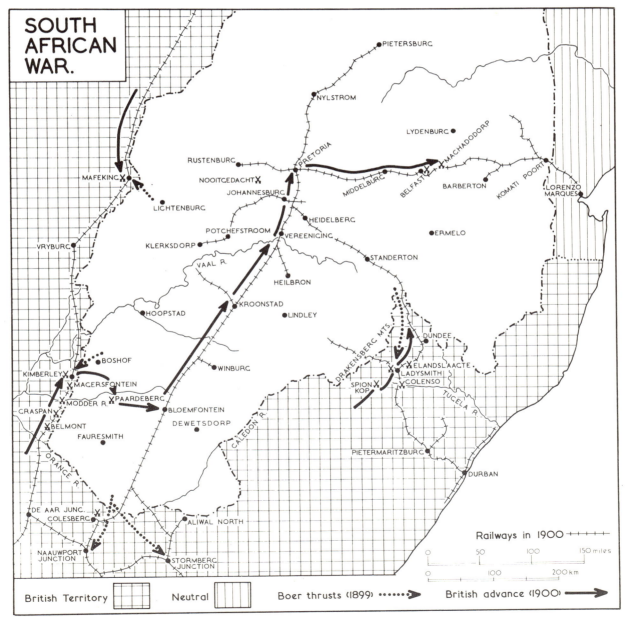

# SOUTH AFRICAN WAR.

PIETERSBURG
NYLSTROM
LYDENBURG
MACHADODORP
MAFEKING
RUSTENBURG
PRETORIA
NOOITGEDACHT
JOHANNESBURG
MIDDELBURG
BELFAST
BARBERTON
KOMATI POORT
LORENZO MARQUES
LICHTENBURG
HEIDELBERG
POTCHEFSTROOM
VEREENIGING
ERMELO
VRYBURG
KLERKSDORP
STANDERTON
VAAL R.
HEILBRON
HOOPSTAD
KROONSTAD
LINDLEY
WINBURG
DUNDEE
BOSHOF
ELANDSLAAGTE
DRAKENSBERG MTS.
KIMBERLEY
MAGERSFONTEIN
SPION KOP
LADYSMITH
COLENSO
MODDER R.
PAARDEBERG
CRASPAN
BELMONT
FAURESMITH
BLOEMFONTEIN
DEWETSDORP
TUGELA R.
CALEDON R.
PIETERMARITZBURG
ORANGE R.
DURBAN
DE AAR JUNC.
COLESBERG
ALIWAL NORTH
NAAUWPORT JUNCTION
STORMBERG JUNCTION

Railways in 1900 ++++++

0   50   100   150 miles
0   100   200 km

British Territory      Neutral      Boer thrusts (1899) ······▶      British advance (1900) ─────▶

27

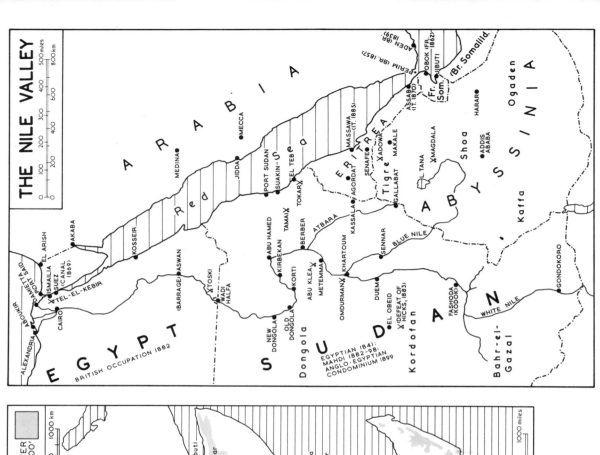

# THE NILE VALLEY

ARABIA

Red Sea

MEDINA●
MECCA●

●JIDDA

PORT SUDAN●
SUAKIN●
EL TEB✗
TOKAR✗
TAMAI✗

MASSAWA●
(IT. 1885)
ASSAB●
(IT. 1870)

PERIM (BR. 1857)
OBOK (FR. 1862)
ADEN (BR. 1839)
JIBUTI●
Fr. Som.
Br. Somalild.

E R I T R E A
SENAFE✗
AGORDAT✗
KASSALA●
KELA✗
BERBER●
AGORDAT✗

Tigre
MAKALE●
XADOWA●
GALLABAT●
XMAGDALA
Shoa
HARAR●
Ogaden

ADDIS ABABA
Kaffa

A B Y S S I N I A

ALEXANDRIA●
ABOUKIR●
PORT SAID●
DAMIETTA●
EL ARISH●
AKABA●
ISMAILIA
SUEZ (CANAL 1869)
CAIRO●
✗TEL-EL-KEBIR
(BARRAGE)
ASWAN●
✗TOSKI
WADI HALFA

KOSSEIR●

NEW DONGOLA
OLD DONGOLA
ABU HAMED●
KIRBEKAN✗
KORTI●
ABU KLEA✗
METEMMA✗

ATBARA●
BERBER●

OMDURMAN✗
KHARTOUM●
DUEM●
SENNAR●
BLUE NILE
L. TANA

EGYPT

BRITISH OCCUPATION 1882

Dongola

EL OBEID●
✗(DEFEAT OF HICKS, 1883)
Kordofan

S U D A N

EGYPTIAN 1841;
MAHDI 1882-98;
ANGLO-EGYPTIAN
CONDOMINIUM 1899

FASHODA (KODOK)●
WHITE NILE

GONDOKORO●

Bahr-el-Gazal

Scale: 0 100 200 300 400 500 miles
0 200 400 600 800 km

---

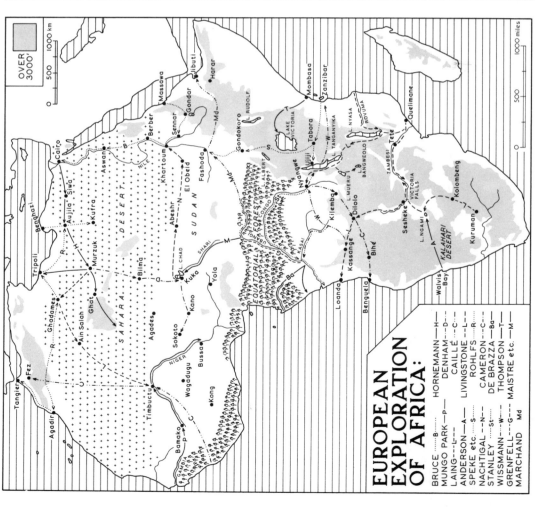

# EUROPEAN EXPLORATION OF AFRICA:

OVER 3000'

Scale: 0 500 1000 km / 0 500 1000 miles

Tangier● Fez●
Agadir●
Tripoli● Benghazi●
Ghadames
Ain Salah●
Ghat
Murzuk● Bilma●
Kufra●
Aujila Siwa●
Cairo●
Aswan●
SAHARA DESERT

Berber●
Sennar●
Gondar●
Massawa●
Jibuti●
Harar●

Abeshr●
El Obeid●
Fashoda●
Khartoum●
Kuka● L. CHAD
SHARI
Yola●
Agades●
Sokoto● Kano●
Bussa●
Wagadugu●
Kong●
Bamako●
Timbuctu●
NIGER
GAMBIA

SUDAN

L. RUDOLF
Gondokoro●
L. ALBERT
LAKE VICTORIA
Mombasa●
Zanzibar
Tabora●
Ujiji●
Nyangwe●
L. TANGANYIKA
L. NYASA
ROVUMA
Quelimane●
Tete●
EQUATORIAL FOREST
CONGO
KASAI
Kilemba●
L. MWERU●
L. BANGWEOLO
Dilolo●
Kassange●
Bihé●
Loanda●
Benguela●
ZAMBESI
VICTORIA FALLS
Sesheke●
L. NGAMI
KALAHARI DESERT
Kuruman●
Kolombeng●
Walvis Bay●

BRUCE --------- B
MUNGO PARK --- P
LAING ---------- L
ANDERSON ----- A
SPEKE etc. ------ S
NACHTIGAL ----- N
STANLEY ------- w
WISSMANN ----- w
GRENFELL ------ G
MARCHAND ----- Md
HORNEMANN --- H
DENHAM ------- D
CAILLÉ -------- C
LIVINGSTONE -- L
ROHLFS ------- R
CAMERON ----- C
DE BRAZZA ---- Ba
THOMPSON ---- T
MAISTRE etc. -- M

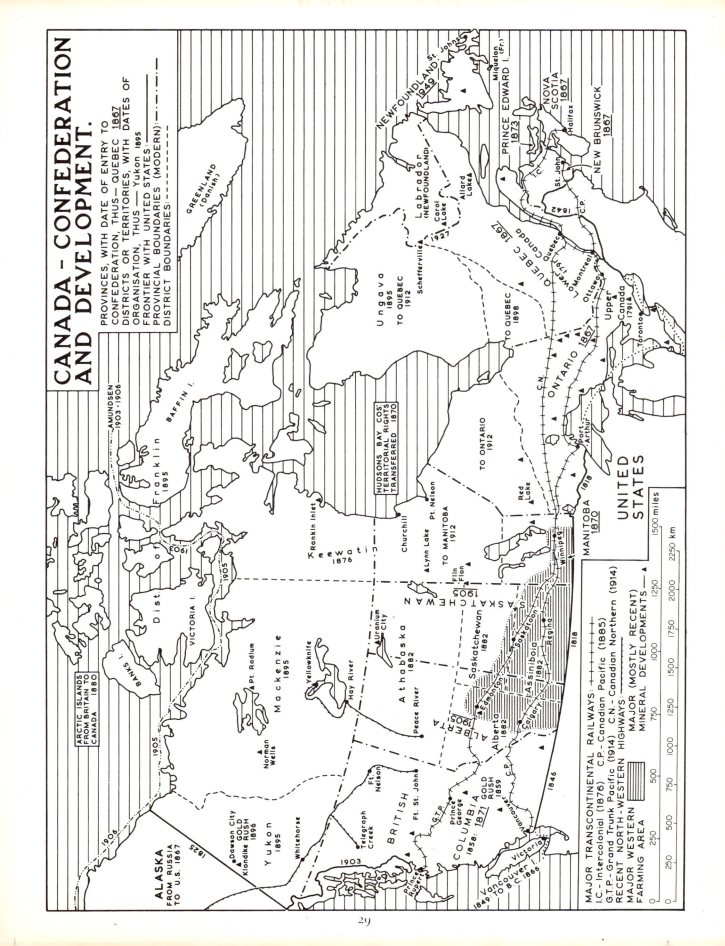

# CANADA – CONFEDERATION AND DEVELOPMENT.

PROVINCES, WITH DATE OF ENTRY TO CONFEDERATION, THUS – QUEBEC 1867
DISTRICTS OR TERRITORIES, WITH DATES OF ORGANISATION, THUS – Yukon 1895
FRONTIER WITH UNITED STATES: ············
PROVINCIAL BOUNDARIES (MODERN): ─ ─ ─ ─
DISTRICT BOUNDARIES: ─·─·─·─·

GREENLAND
(Danish)

AMUNDSEN 1903-1906

Franklin 1895
BAFFIN I.

Dist. of Franklin

1903

1905

VICTORIA I.

BANKS I.

1825
1906

ALASKA
FROM RUSSIA TO U.S. 1867

Dawson City
Klondike GOLD RUSH 1896
Whitehorse
Y u k o n 1895

Telegraph Creek
1903

Prince Rupert
1849 TO B.C. 1866
BRITISH COLUMBIA 1858: 1871

Ft. Nelson
Ft. St. John
G.T.P.
Prince George
GOLD RUSH 1859
Vancouver
Victoria

Pt. Radium
M a c k e n z i e 1895
Norman Wells
Yellowknife
Hay River

Uranium City
A t h a b a s k a 1882
Peace River
ALBERTA 1882: 1905
Edmonton
Calgary
C.P.

K e e w a t i n 1876

Rankin Inlet

Churchill
Flin Flon
Lynn Lake
TO MANITOBA 1912
Pt. Nelson

SASKATCHEWAN 1882: 1905
Saskatoon
Assiniboia 1882
Regina

MANITOBA 1870
Winnipeg
Red Lake

1818

1846

UNITED STATES

HUDSONS BAY COS. TERRITORIAL RIGHTS TRANSFERRED 1870

U n g a v a 1895 TO QUEBEC 1912

Schefferville 1927

TO QUEBEC 1898

TO ONTARIO 1912

TO ONTARIO

Labrador (NEWFOUNDLAND)
Carol Lake
Allard Lake

NEWFOUNDLAND 1949
St. Johns
Miquelon (Fr.)
St. Pierre (Fr.)

PRINCE EDWARD I. 1873
T.C.
St. John
1842
C.P.
Halifax
NOVA SCOTIA 1867
NEW BRUNSWICK 1867

QUEBEC 1867
Lower Canada 1791
Quebec
Montreal
Ottawa
C.N.
ONTARIO 1867
Upper Canada 1791
Toronto
Port Arthur

ARCTIC ISLANDS FROM BRITAIN TO CANADA 1880

MAJOR TRANSCONTINENTAL RAILWAYS:
I.C.– Intercolonial (1876)    C.P.– Canadian Pacific (1885)
G.T.P.– Grand Trunk Pacific (1914)    C.N.– Canadian Northern (1914)
RECENT NORTH-WESTERN HIGHWAYS: _____
MAJOR (MOSTLY RECENT) MINERAL DEVELOPMENTS ▲
MAJOR WESTERN FARMING AREA |||||

0    250    500    750    1000    1250    1500 miles
0    250    500    750    1000    1250    1500    1750    2000    2250 km

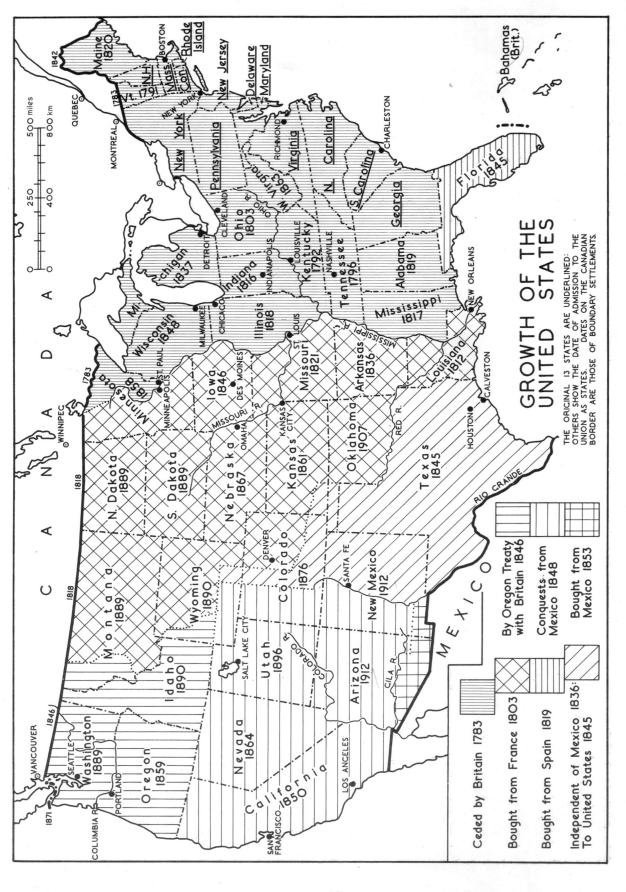

GROWTH OF THE UNITED STATES

THE ORIGINAL 13 STATES ARE UNDERLINED:
OTHERS SHOW THE DATE OF ADMISSION TO THE
UNION AS STATES. DATES ON THE CANADIAN
BORDER ARE THOSE OF BOUNDARY SETTLEMENTS.

Ceded by Britain 1783

Bought from France 1803

Bought from Spain 1819

Independent of Mexico 1836:
To United States 1845

By Oregon Treaty
with Britain 1846

Conquests from
Mexico 1848

Bought from
Mexico 1853

The coastline of Mississippi and Alabama was disputed by Spain until 1819.   The western half of Texas was disputed by Mexico until the war of 1846-8.   West
Virginia became separate from Virginia during the Civil War.

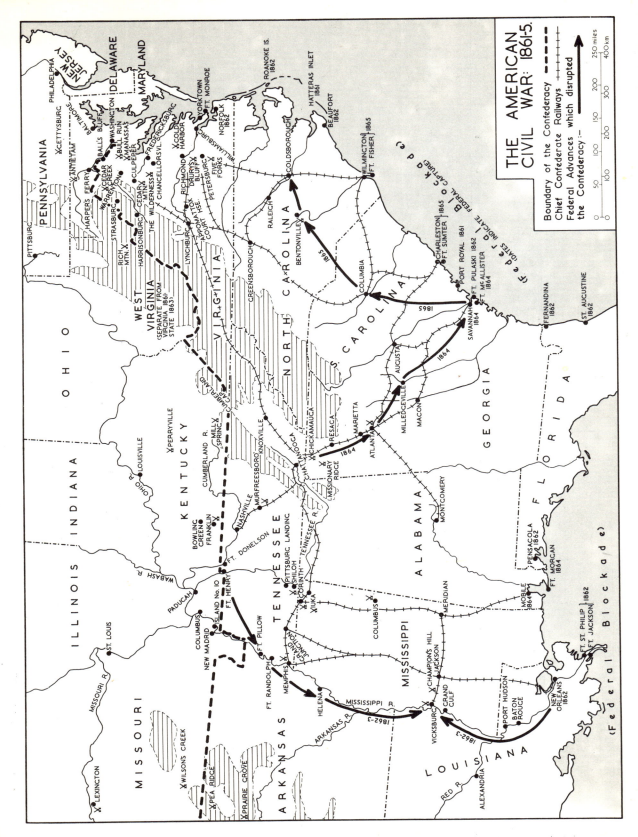

THE AMERICAN CIVIL WAR: 1861-5.

Boundary of the Confederacy ▬▬
Chief Confederate Railways ┼┼┼┼┼
Federal Advances which disrupted
the Confederacy :-

Maryland, West Virginia, Kentucky, Missouri, and Kansas were divided in sympathy, and joined the Federal cause only after their occupation by Federal forces. Texas (not shown) was an important member of the Confederacy. Land over 1000 feet indicated by lines.

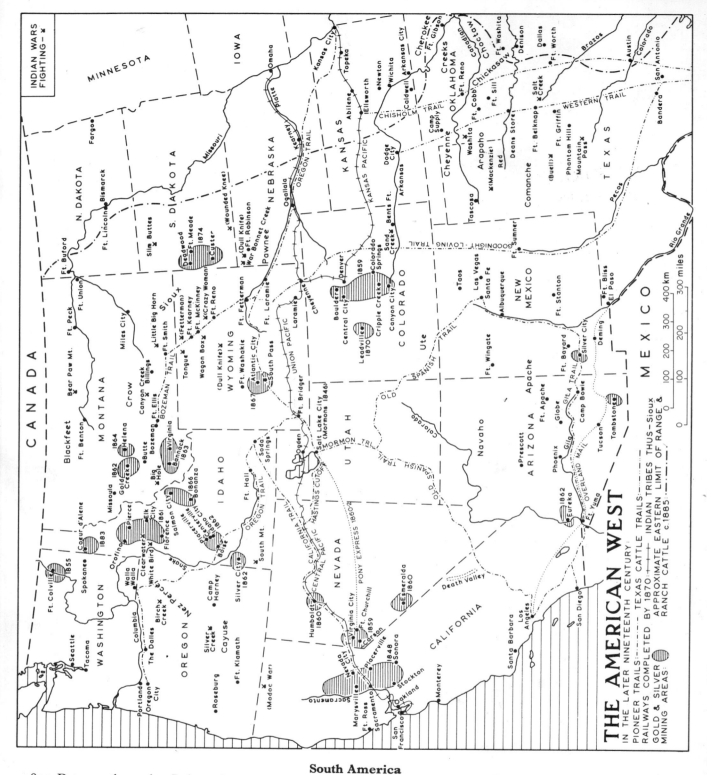

**South America**

1825: Dates are those when Independence was established: its declaration sometimes preceded this by several years. Mexico and Central America became independent in 1821, and separate federal republics in 1823. The latter split into its present divisions in 1839.

1948: By the peace of 1883 the Tacna-Arica area went to Chile provisionally: a plebiscite due in 1893 was not held, and Chile kept possession. Tacna was restored to Peru in 1929.

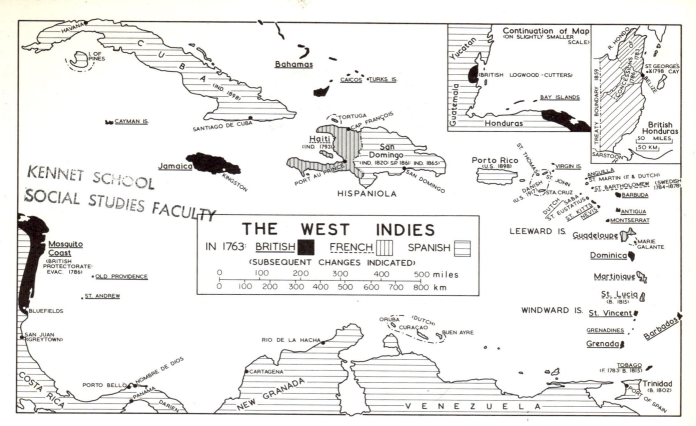

HAVANA

I. OF PINES

C U B A

Bahamas

CAICOS · TURKS IS.

(IND. 1898)

CAYMAN IS.

SANTIAGO DE CUBA

TORTUGA

CAP FRANÇOIS

KENNET SCHOOL
SOCIAL STUDIES FACULTY

Haiti
(IND. 1793)

San Domingo
(IND. 1820: SP 1861: IND. 1865)

Jamaica

KINGSTON

PORT AU PRINCE

SAN DOMINGO

HISPANIOLA

Porto Rico
(U.S. 1898)

ST. THOMAS

VIRGIN IS.

ANGUILLA

ST. MARTIN (F. & DUTCH)

ST. JOHN

DANISH
(U.S. 1917)

STA. CRUZ

ST. BARTHOLOMEW
(SWEDISH 1784-1878)

DUTCH
SABA

BARBUDA

ST. EUSTATIUS
ST. KITTS
NEVIS

ANTIGUA

MONTSERRAT

LEEWARD IS.

Guadeloupe

MARIE GALANTE

Dominica

Martinique

St. Lucia
(B. 1815)

WINDWARD IS.

St. Vincent

Barbados

GRENADINES

Grenada

TOBAGO
(F. 1783: B. 1815)

Trinidad
(B. 1802)

PORT OF SPAIN

Mosquito Coast
(BRITISH PROTECTORATE: EVAC. 1786)

OLD PROVIDENCE

ST. ANDREW

BLUEFIELDS

SAN JUAN
(GREYTOWN)

COSTA RICA

PORTO BELLO

NOMBRE DE DIOS

PANAMA

DARIEN

CARTAGENA

NEW GRANADA

RIO DE LA HACHA

ORUBA
CURAÇAO
(DUTCH)

BUEN AYRE

V E N E Z U E L A

**Continuation of Map**
(ON SLIGHTLY SMALLER SCALE)

Yucatan

(BRITISH LOGWOOD-CUTTERS)

Guatemala

BAY ISLANDS

Honduras

R. HONDO

TREATY BOUNDARY 1859

CONCESSIONS OF 1783
1786

ST. GEORGE'S
×1798 CAY
BELIZE

British Honduras

SARSTOON

50 MILES
50 KM

## THE WEST INDIES
IN 1763: BRITISH ■ FRENCH ▥ SPANISH ▤

(SUBSEQUENT CHANGES INDICATED)

0   100   200   300   400   500 miles
0  100 200 300 400 500 600 700 800 km

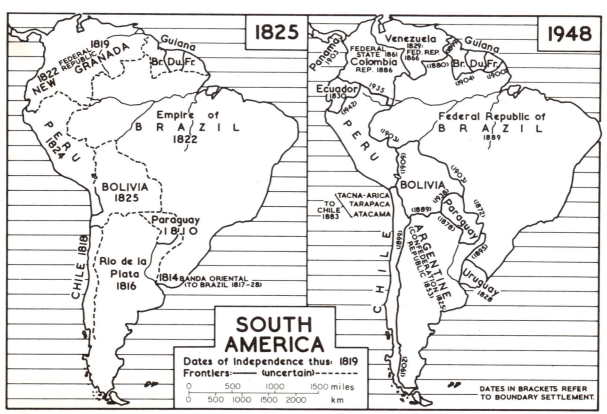

### 1825

1819

FEDERAL REPUBLIC

1822

NEW GRANADA

Guiana
Br. Du. Fr.

P E R U
1824

Empire of
B R A Z I L
1822

BOLIVIA
1825

Paraguay
1810

CHILE 1818

Rio de la Plata
1816

1814 BANDA ORIENTAL
(TO BRAZIL 1817-28)

### 1948

Panama
1903

Venezuela
1829:
FED. REP.
1866

FEDERAL
STATE 1861
Colombia
REP. 1886

Guiana
Br. Du. Fr.

(1880)
(1904)
(1900)

Ecuador
1830

1935

1942

P E R U

C H I L E

TACNA-ARICA
TARAPACA
ATACAMA
TO CHILE 1883

BOLIVIA

Federal Republic of
B R A Z I L
1889

(1899)

(1889)
(1938)
(1878)

Paraguay
(1872)
(1893)

ARGENTINE
(CONFEDERATION)
(REPUBLIC 1853)

Uruguay
1828

DATES IN BRACKETS REFER
TO BOUNDARY SETTLEMENT.

## SOUTH AMERICA
Dates of Independence thus: 1819
Frontiers: —— (uncertain) ------

0      500     1000    1500 miles
0   500 1000 1500 2000 km

(See note on opposite page.)

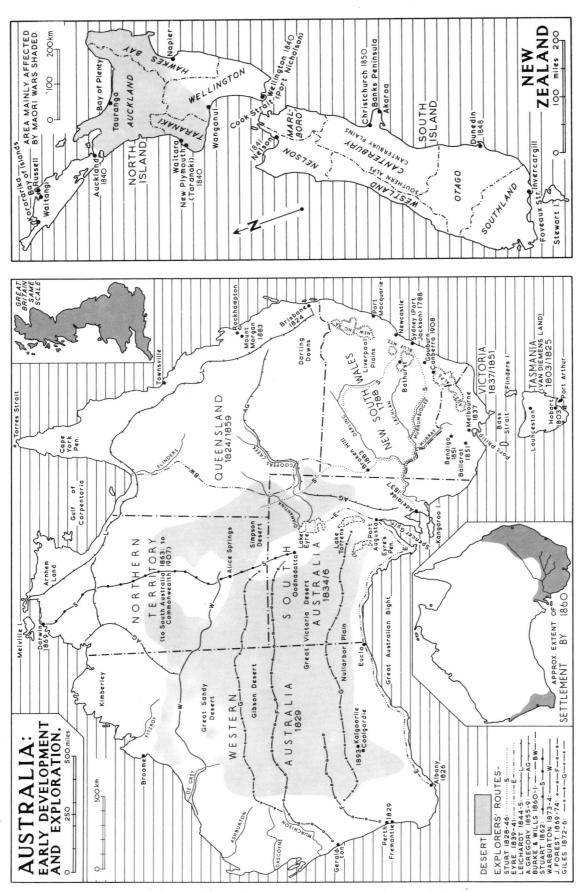

## NEW ZEALAND

AREA MAINLY AFFECTED
BY MAORI WARS SHADED.

0   100   200km

NORTH ISLAND

Kororarika Bay of Islands
Russell
Waitangi
Auckland 1840
Bay of Plenty
Tauranga
AUCKLAND
Napier
HAWKES BAY
WELLINGTON
TARANAKI
New Plymouth (Taranaki) 1840
Waitara 1840
Wanganui
Wellington 1840 (Port Nicholson)
Cook Strait
N.1841
Nelson
MARL-BORO

SOUTH ISLAND

NELSON
CANTERBURY
WESTLAND
SOUTHERN ALPS
Christchurch 1850
Banks Peninsula
Akaroa
Canterbury Plains
OTAGO
Dunedin 1848
SOUTHLAND
Invercargill
Foveaux Str.
Stewart I.

0   100   200
miles

## AUSTRALIA: EARLY DEVELOPMENT AND EXPLORATION.

GREAT BRITAIN SAME SCALE

500 miles
0   250
0   500km

Torres Strait
Cape York Pen.
Gulf of Carpentaria
Arnhem Land
Melville I.
Darwin 1869
Kimberley
Broome
FITZROY
DE GREY
ASHBURTON
MURCHISON
GASCOYNE
GERALDTON
Perth 1829
Fremantle 1829

NORTHERN TERRITORY (to South Australia 1863; to Commonwealth 1907)
Alice Springs
Simpson Desert
Great Sandy Desert
Gibson Desert
WESTERN AUSTRALIA 1829
Great Victoria Desert
Kalgoorlie 1893
Coolgardie
Nullarbor Plain
Eucla
Albany 1826

SOUTH AUSTRALIA 1834/6
Oodnadatta
Lake Eyre
Lake Torrens
Port Augusta
Eyre's Pen.
Spencer Gulf
Kangaroo I.
Adelaide 1837
Great Australian Bight

QUEENSLAND 1824/1859
Rockhampton
Mount Morgan 1883
DIAMANTINA
COOPERS CREEK
FLINDERS
Darling Downs
Brisbane 1824

NEW SOUTH WALES 1788
Townsville
Port Macquarie
Newcastle
Sydney (Port Jackson) 1788
Liverpool Plains
BLUE MTS.
Bathurst
Goulburn 1908
Canberra 1908
LACHLAN
DARLING
MURRUMBIDGEE
MURRAY
Broken Hill 1883
Bendigo 1851
Ballarat 1851
Melbourne 1837
Port Phillip
VICTORIA 1837/1851
Bass Strait
Flinders I.

TASMANIA (VAN DIEMENS LAND) 1803/1825
Launceston
Hobart 1803
Port Arthur

APPROX. EXTENT OF SETTLEMENT BY 1860

DESERT

EXPLORERS' ROUTES–
STURT 1828-46: ......... S
EYRE 1839-41: ——E——
LEICHARDT 1844-5: ——AG——
A. GREGORY 1855-9: ——BW——
BURKE & WILLS 1860-1: ——S——
STUART 1862: ——W——
WARBURTON 1873-4: ——F——
J. FOREST 1869-74: ——G——
GILES 1872-6: —+—+—

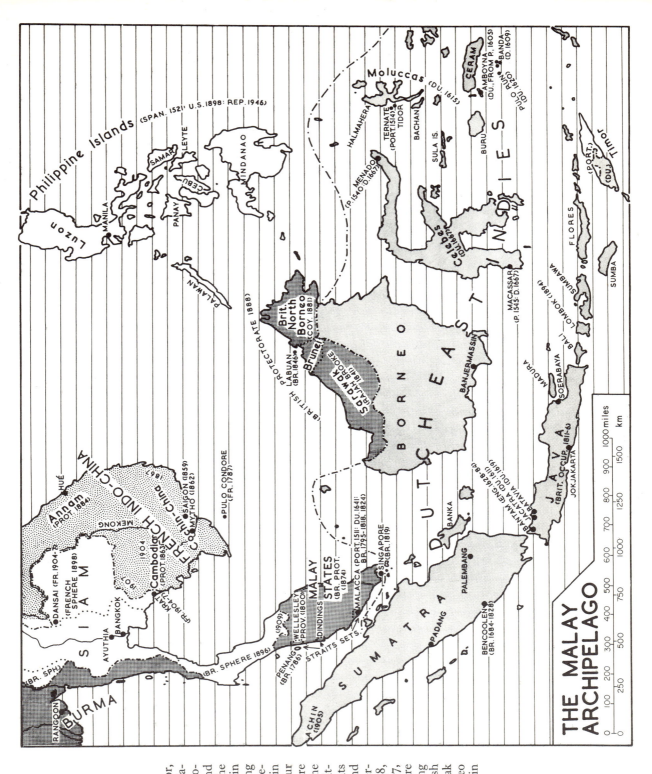

THE MALAY ARCHIPELAGO

In Malaya, Perak, Selangor, Pahang accepted British protection between 1874 and 1889, and became the Federated Malay States in 1895. Of the remaining Malay States, Johore became a protectorate in 1885, and the other four when Siamese claims were abandoned in 1909. The Malay States and the British Straits Settlements colonies of Penang and Malacca became the Federation of Malaya in 1948, and independent in 1957, at which date Singapore also became self-governing though remaining a British military base. Sarawak and British North Borneo became Crown Colonies in 1946.

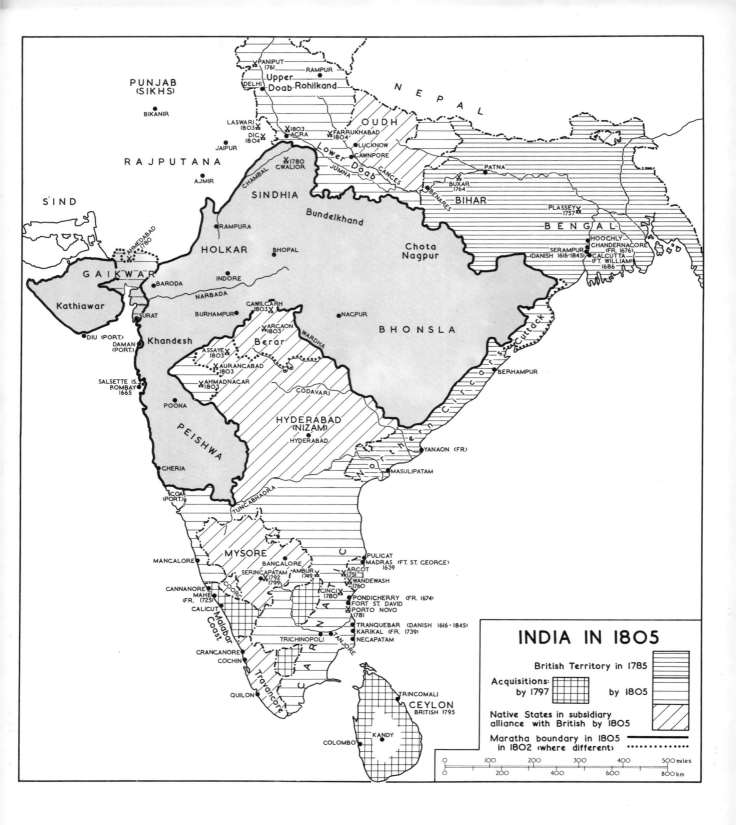

PUNJAB
(SIKHS)

BIKANIR

RAJPUTANA

AJMIR
JAIPUR

SIND

S I N D

GAIKWAR

Kathiawar

AHMEDABAD
1780

BARODA

SURAT

DIU (PORT.)
DAMAN
(PORT.)

Khandesh

SALSETTE IS.
BOMBAY
1665

POONA

PEISHWA

CHERIA

GOA
(PORT.)

MANGALORE

CANNANORE
MAHE
(FR. 1725)

CALICUT

Malabar Coast

CRANGANORE

COCHIN

QUILON

Travancore

N E P A L

PANIPUT
1761

RAMPUR

DELHI

Upper Doab
Rohilkand

LASWARI
1803

DIC
1804

AGRA
1803

FARRUKHABAD
1804

OUDH

LUCKNOW
CAWNPORE

GWALIOR
1780

SINDHIA

CHAMBAL

Lower Doab

JUMNA

GANGES

PATNA

BUXAR
1764

BENARES

BIHAR

PLASSEY
1757

B E N G A L

HOOGHLY
CHANDERNAGORE
(FR. 1676)
SERAMPUR
(DANISH 1616-1845)
CALCUTTA
(FT. WILLIAM)
1686

RAMPURA

HOLKAR

BHOPAL

INDORE

Bundelkhand

Chota
Nagpur

NARBADA

BURHAMPUR

CAWILGARH
1803

VARGAON
1803

Berar

ASSAYE
1803

AURANGABAD
1803

AHMADNAGAR
1803

WARDHA

NACPUR

B H O N S L A

Cuttack

BERHAMPUR

CODAVARI

HYDERABAD
(NIZAM)

HYDERABAD

YANAON (FR.)

MASULIPATAM

TUNCABHADRA

MYSORE

BANGALORE

SERINGAPATAM
1792
1799

AMBUR
1749

COORG

PULICAT
MADRAS (FT. ST. GEORGE)
1639

ARCOT
1751

WANDEWASH
1760

CINCIX
1780

PONDICHERRY (FR. 1674)
FORT ST. DAVID
PORTO NOVO
1781

TRANQUEBAR (DANISH 1616-1845)
KARIKAL (FR. 1739)

NECAPATAM

TRICHINOPOLI

TANJORE

TRINCOMALI

CEYLON
BRITISH 1795

COLOMBO

KANDY

## INDIA IN 1805

British Territory in 1785

Acquisitions:
by 1797          by 1805

Native States in subsidiary
alliance with British by 1805

Maratha boundary in 1805 ————
in 1802 (where different) ·········

| 0 | 100 | 200 | 300 | 400 | 500 miles |

| 0 | 200 | 400 | 600 | 800 km |

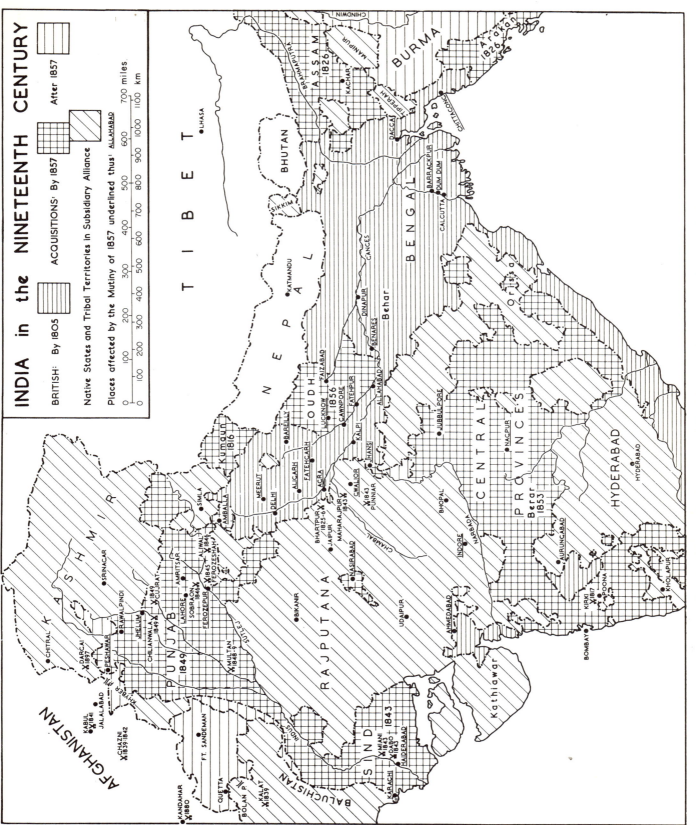

## INDIA in the NINETEENTH CENTURY

BRITISH:  By 1805    ACQUISITIONS:  By 1857    After 1857

Native States and Tribal Territories in Subsidiary Alliance

Places affected by the Mutiny of 1857 underlined thus: ALLAHABAD

0   100   200   300   400   500   600   700 miles
0  100  200  300  400  500  600  700  800  900 1000 1100  km

AFGHANISTAN

KABUL X1841
JALALABAD
GHAZNI X1839-1842
KANDAHAR X1880

KHYBER P.
CHITRAL
DARCAI X1897
PESHAWAR
RAWALPINDI
KASHMIR
SRINAGAR
JHELUM
CHILIANWALA X1849
GUJRAT X1849
LAHORE
AMRITSAR
ALIWAL X1846
SOBRAON 1846
FEROZEPUR
FEROZESHAH X1845
MULTAN 1848-9
PUNJAB 1849

FT. SANDEMAN
QUETTA
BOLAN P.
KALAT X1839
BALUCHISTAN

SIND 1843
KARACHI X
HAIDERABAD
MIANI X1843
DABO X1843

RAJPUTANA
BIKANIR
NASIRABAD
JAIPUR
UDAIPUR
1843

TIBET
LHASA

KUMAUN 1816
SIMLA
AMBALLA
MEERUT
DELHI
ALIGARH
FATEHGARH
AGRA
BHARTPUR 1825-6 X
MAHARAJPUR X1843
PUNNIAR X1843
GWALIOR
CHAMBAL

NEPAL
KATMANDU

BHUTAN

SIKKIM

ASSAM 1826
BRAHMAPUTRA
KACHAR
MANIPUR
TIPPERAH

BURMA
CHINDWIN
Arakan 1826

OUDH
LUCKNOW
CAWNPORE
FATEHPUR
ALLAHABAD
KALPI
HANS
FAIZABAD
BAREILLY
1856

BENARES
DINAPUR
Behar
CANCES

BENGAL
DACCA
BARRACKPUR
DUM DUM
CALCUTTA
CHITTAGONG

Orissa

CENTRAL PROVINCES
JUBBULPORE
NAGPUR
Berar 1853
BHOPAL
NARBADA
INDORE
AURUNGABAD

HYDERABAD
HYDERABAD

Kathiawar
AHMEDABAD
BOMBAY
KIRKI X1817
POONA
KHOLAPUR

(For the French, Portuguese, and Danish possessions, see previous map.)

37

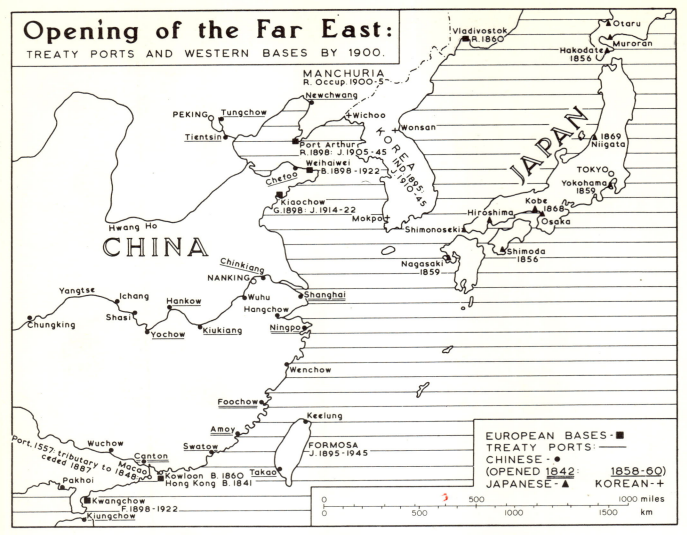

# Opening of the Far East:
## TREATY PORTS AND WESTERN BASES BY 1900.

MANCHURIA
R. Occup. 1900-5

Newchwang
PEKING    Tungchow
Tientsin
+Wichoo
+Wonsan
Vladivostok R.1860
Otaru
Muroran
Hakodate 1856

Port Arthur
R.1898: J.1905-45
Weihaiwei
B.1898-1922
Chefoo
Kiaochow
G.1898: J.1914-22
Mokpo
Shimonoseki

KOREA IND.1895
J.1910-45

JAPAN

1869 Niigata
TOKYO
Yokohama 1859
Kobe 1868
Hiroshima
Osaka

Hwang Ho

CHINA

Chinkiang
NANKING
Yangtse
Ichang
Hankow
Shasi
Yochow
Kiukiang
Chungking
Wuhu
Hangchow
Shanghai
Ningpo
Nagasaki 1859
Shimoda 1856

Wenchow

Foochow

Amoy
Swatow
Keelung
FORMOSA
J.1895-1945

Wuchow
Canton
Port.1557: tributary to 1848: ceded 1887
Macao
Pakhoi
Kowloon B.1860
Hong Kong B.1841
Takao

Kwangchow
F.1898-1922
Kiungchow

EUROPEAN BASES - ■
TREATY PORTS: —
CHINESE - ●
(OPENED 1842:   1858-60)
JAPANESE - ▲    KOREAN - +

0    500    1000 miles
0    500    1000    1500 km

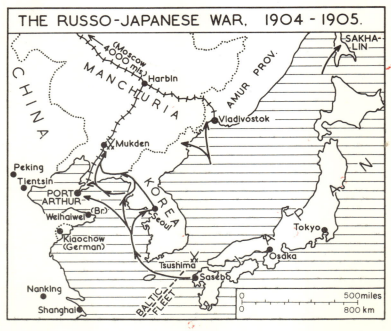

# THE RUSSO-JAPANESE WAR, 1904-1905.

(Moscow 4000 mls)
CHINA
MANCHURIA
Harbin
SAKHALIN
AMUR PROV.
Vladivostok
Mukden
Peking
Tientsin
PORT ARTHUR
(Br.)
Weihaiwei
Kiaochow (German)
Seoul
KOREA
Tsushima
Tokyo
Osaka
Sasebo
Nanking
Shanghai
BALTIC FLEET

0    500 miles
0    800 km

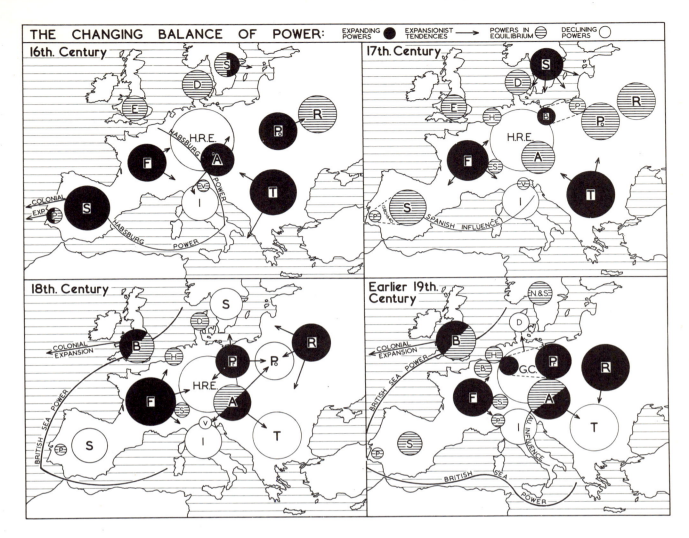

THE CHANGING BALANCE OF POWER: EXPANDING POWERS ● EXPANSIONIST TENDENCIES → POWERS IN EQUILIBRIUM ⊖ DECLINING POWERS ○

These diagrams are intended to give an overall picture of the European Balance of Power at various periods, and to illustrate the changes in the Balance and in the relative political importance of individual states.

39

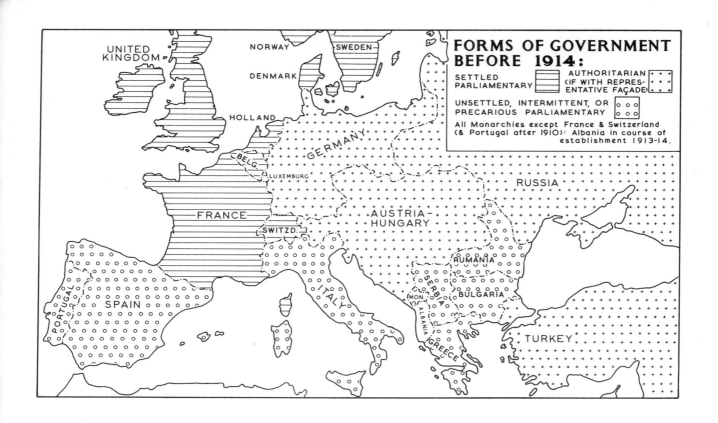

## FORMS OF GOVERNMENT BEFORE 1914:

SETTLED PARLIAMENTARY

AUTHORITARIAN (IF WITH REPRESENTATIVE FAÇADE)

UNSETTLED, INTERMITTENT, OR PRECARIOUS PARLIAMENTARY

All Monarchies except France & Switzerland (& Portugal after 1910): Albania in course of establishment 1913-14.

UNITED KINGDOM

NORWAY

SWEDEN

DENMARK

HOLLAND

GERMANY

BELG.

LUXEMBURG

RUSSIA

FRANCE

SWITZD.

AUSTRIA-HUNGARY

ITALY

RUMANIA

SERBIA

MON.

ALBANIA

BULGARIA

GREECE

PORTUGAL

SPAIN

TURKEY

# EMPIRES IN 1914 — COMPARATIVE AREA

**WEST EUROPEAN**
Metropolitan Country shown in black

**CONTINENTAL**
for comparison

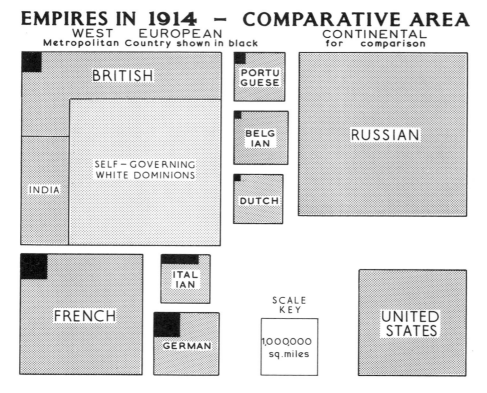

BRITISH

PORTUGUESE

BELGIAN

RUSSIAN

INDIA

SELF-GOVERNING WHITE DOMINIONS

DUTCH

FRENCH

ITALIAN

GERMAN

SCALE KEY

1,000,000 sq.miles

UNITED STATES

40

# FIRST WORLD WAR:

ENLISTMENTS & CASUALTIES IN MAJOR EUROPEAN STATES, IN MILLIONS

WOUNDED

KILLED

RUSSIA

GERMANY

FRANCE

AUSTRIA

UNITED KINGDOM

ITALY

11 — 10 — 9 — 8 — 7 — 6 — 5 — 4 — 3 — 2 — 1 —

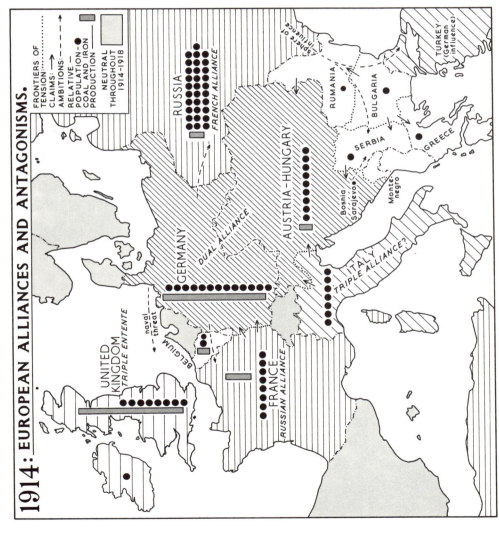

# 1914: EUROPEAN ALLIANCES AND ANTAGONISMS.

FRONTIERS OF TENSION:
CLAIMS:
AMBITIONS:
RELATIVE — POPULATION —
COAL AND IRON PRODUCTION
NEUTRAL THROUGHOUT 1914-1918

RUSSIA

FRENCH ALLIANCE

GERMANY

DUAL ALLIANCE

AUSTRIA-HUNGARY

RUMANIA

BULGARIA

SERBIA

GREECE

Bosnia
Sarajevo

Monte negro

sphere of influence

TURKEY
(German influence)

ITALY
TRIPLE ALLIANCE?

UNITED KINGDOM
TRIPLE ENTENTE

naval threat

BELGIUM

FRANCE
RUSSIAN ALLIANCE

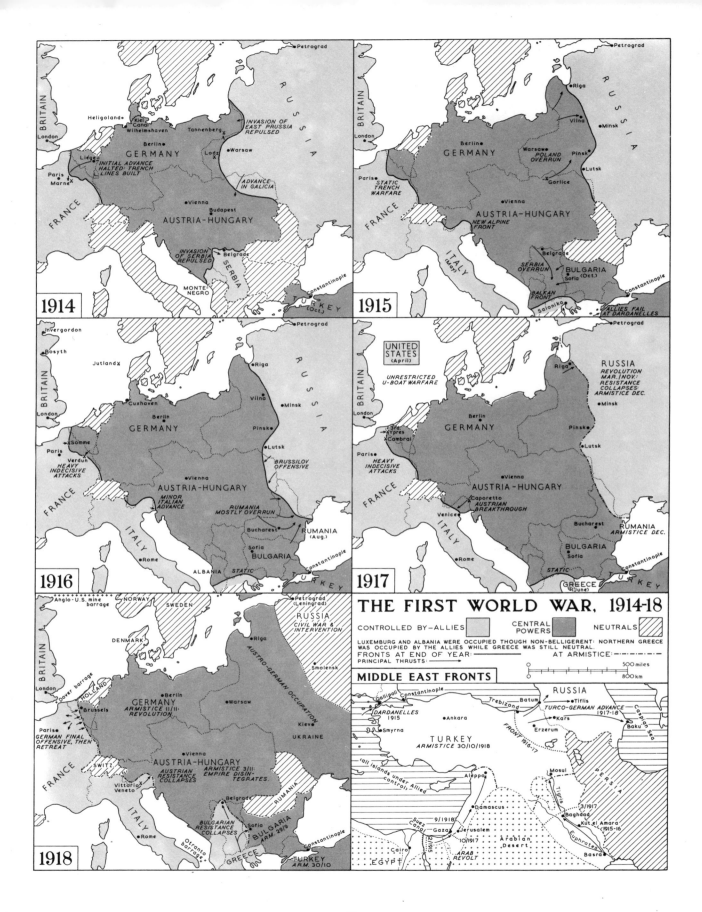

## 1914

BRITAIN
London
Heligoland
Kiel Canal
Wilhelmshaven
Berlin
GERMANY
Liège
INITIAL ADVANCE
HALTED: TRENCH
LINES BUILT
Paris
Marne
FRANCE
Vienna
Budapest
AUSTRIA–HUNGARY
Tannenberg
INVASION OF
EAST PRUSSIA
REPULSED
Lodz
Warsaw
RUSSIA
ADVANCE
IN GALICIA
INVASION
OF SERBIA
REPULSED
Belgrade
SERBIA
MONTE
NEGRO
Petrograd
Constantinople
TURKEY
(Oct.)

## 1915

BRITAIN
London
Paris
STATIC
TRENCH
WARFARE
FRANCE
GERMANY
Berlin
ITALY
(May)
AUSTRIA–HUNGARY
NEW ALPINE
FRONT
Vienna
Warsaw
POLAND
OVERRUN
Gorlice
Belgrade
SERBIA
OVERRUN
BALKAN
FRONT
BULGARIA
Sofia (Oct.)
Salonika
Riga
Vilna
Minsk
Pinsk
Lutsk
RUSSIA
Petrograd
Constantinople
ALLIES FAIL
AT DARDANELLES

## 1916

Invergordon
Rosyth
Jutland x
BRITAIN
London
Cuxhaven
Berlin
GERMANY
Paris
x Somme
Verdun
HEAVY
INDECISIVE
ATTACKS
FRANCE
Vienna
AUSTRIA–HUNGARY
MINOR
ITALIAN
ADVANCE
ITALY
Rome
ALBANIA
STATIC
Vilna
Minsk
Pinsk
Lutsk
BRUSSILOV
OFFENSIVE
RUMANIA
MOSTLY OVERRUN
Bucharest
RUMANIA
(Aug.)
Sofia
BULGARIA
Constantinople
TURKEY
Riga
RUSSIA
Petrograd

## 1917

UNITED
STATES
(April)
UNRESTRICTED
U-BOAT WARFARE
BRITAIN
London
Paris
HEAVY
INDECISIVE
ATTACKS
FRANCE
3rd
Ypres
Cambrai
Berlin
GERMANY
Vienna
AUSTRIA–HUNGARY
Caporetto
Venice
AUSTRIAN
BREAKTHROUGH
ITALY
Rome
STATIC
GREECE
(June)
Bucharest
BULGARIA
Sofia
Constantinople
TURKEY
Riga
Minsk
Pinsk
Lutsk
RUSSIA
REVOLUTION
MAR. [NOV.]
RESISTANCE
COLLAPSES:
ARMISTICE DEC.
RUMANIA
ARMISTICE DEC.
Petrograd

## 1918

Anglo-U.S. mine
barrage
NORWAY
SWEDEN
DENMARK
BRITAIN
London
Dover barrage
HOLLAND
Brussels
Paris
GERMAN FINAL
OFFENSIVE, THEN
RETREAT
FRANCE
SWITZ.
Berlin
GERMANY
ARMISTICE 11/11:
REVOLUTION
Warsaw
Kiev
UKRAINE
AUSTRO-GERMAN OCCUPATION
Vienna
AUSTRIA–HUNGARY
AUSTRIAN
RESISTANCE
COLLAPSES
ARMISTICE 3/11:
EMPIRE DISIN-
TEGRATES.
Vittorio
Veneto
ITALY
Rome
Otranto
barrage
Belgrade
BULGARIAN
RESISTANCE
COLLAPSES
Sofia
BULGARIA
ARM. 29/9
GREECE
Constantinople
TURKEY
ARM. 30/10
RUMANIA
Petrograd
(Leningrad)
RUSSIA
CIVIL WAR &
INTERVENTION
Riga
Smolensk

# THE FIRST WORLD WAR, 1914-18

CONTROLLED BY–ALLIES    CENTRAL POWERS    NEUTRALS

LUXEMBURG AND ALBANIA WERE OCCUPIED THOUGH NON-BELLIGERENT: NORTHERN GREECE
WAS OCCUPIED BY THE ALLIES WHILE GREECE WAS STILL NEUTRAL.
FRONTS AT END OF YEAR:⸺ AT ARMISTICE:⸺
PRINCIPAL THRUSTS:⸺

0    500 miles
0    800 km

## MIDDLE EAST FRONTS

Gallipoli    Constantinople
DARDANELLES
1915
Smyrna
Ankara
TURKEY
ARMISTICE 30/10/1918
all islands under Allied
control
Suez
Canal
9/1918
Gaza
10/1917
2/1915
Jerusalem
Cairo
EGYPT
Arabian
Desert
ARAB
REVOLT
Trebizond
Batum
RUSSIA
Tiflis
TURCO-GERMAN ADVANCE
1917-18
Kars
Erzerum
FRONT 1916-17
Baku
Caspian Sea
Aleppo
Damascus
Mosul
Tigris
3/1917
Baghdad
Kut el Amara
1915-16
Euphrates
Basra
PERSIA

RUSSIA 1918-20
POST-REVOLUTIONARY
CIVIL WAR AND INTER-
VENTION CRISIS.

APPROXIMATE FURTHEST PENETRATION
OF WHITE RUSSIAN AND INTERVENTION
FORCES 1919 (NOT SIMULTANEOUS) THUS:

Murmansk

WHITE SEA

Kem

Archangel

FINLAND
10/1920

ALLIED INTERVENTION

Shenkursk
Kotlas

Tobolsk

FINNS

Vyatka

Perm

Ekaterinburg

Vologda

WHITES &
CZECHS

Petrograd

Chelyab-
insk

BRITISH
NAVY

ESTONIA
2/1920

Yaroslavl

Kazan

Ufa

Trans-Siberian Railway

Pskov

BALTIC SEA

LATVIA
8/1920

Moscow

Simbirsk

Orenburg

LITHUANIA
7/1920

Vitebsk

Smolensk

Tula

Uralsk

Minsk

Orel

Saratov

POLAND
10/1920

Gomel

Kursk

Voronezh

POLES

Kharkov

WHITES WITH
ALLIED SUPPORT

Don

Tsaritsin

Volga

Astrakhan

Kiev

UKRAINE
(separatist 1918-20)

Ekaterinoslav

Rostov

0        500 km

Odessa

CASPIAN SEA

RUSSIAN FRONTIER
1914:
1921:

DATES OF TREATIES
BETWEEN U.S.S.R. AND
NEIGHBOURING STATES
THUS: 10/1920.

0      200  miles  400

Sebastopol

ALLIED NAVIES

BLACK SEA

Grozny

Vladikavkaz

Tiflis

Batum

TRANSCAUCASIA
(separatist 1918-20)

Baku

Kars

TURKEY 10/1920

TURKS

BRITISH

43

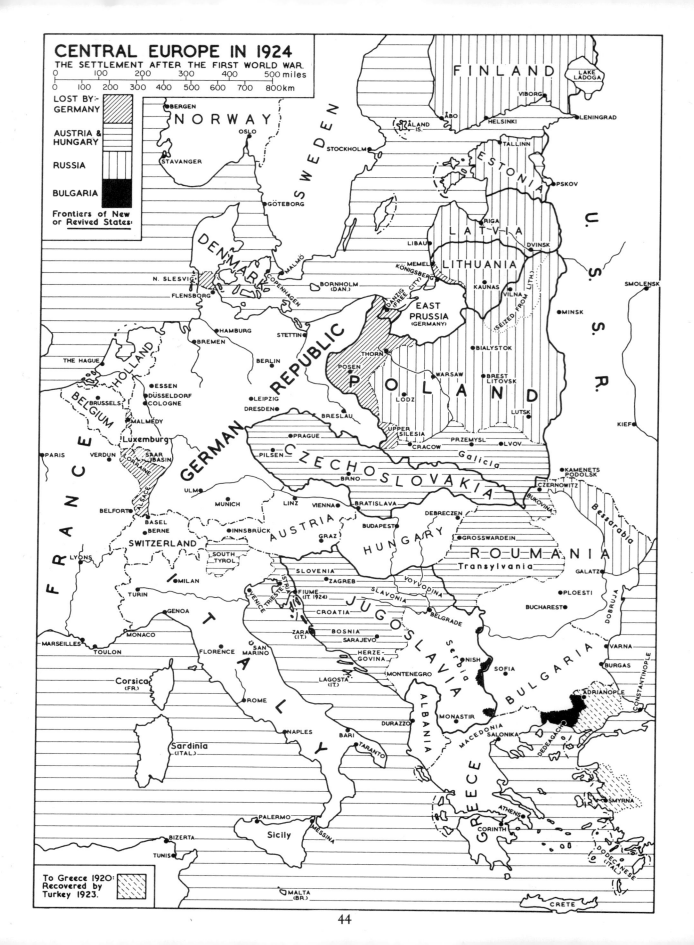

# CENTRAL EUROPE IN 1924

THE SETTLEMENT AFTER THE FIRST WORLD WAR.

0    100    200    300    400    500 miles
0    100    200    300    400    500    600    700    800km

LOST BY:-
GERMANY

AUSTRIA &
HUNGARY

RUSSIA

BULGARIA

Frontiers of New
or Revived States:

NORWAY
BERGEN
OSLO
STAVANGER

SWEDEN
GÖTEBORG
STOCKHOLM

FINLAND
ÅBO
ÅLAND IS.
HELSINKI
VIBORG
LAKE LADOGA
LENINGRAD

ESTONIA
TALLINN
PSKOV

LATVIA
RIGA
LIBAU
DVINSK

U.S.S.R.
SMOLENSK

DENMARK
N. SLESVIG
FLENSBORG
COPENHAGEN
MALMÖ
BORNHOLM (DAN.)

LITHUANIA
MEMEL
KÖNIGSBERG
DANZIG (FREE CITY)
KAUNAS
VILNA
(SEIZED FROM LITH.)
MINSK

EAST PRUSSIA (GERMANY)

HOLLAND
THE HAGUE

BELGIUM
BRUSSELS
MALMÉDY

HAMBURG
BREMEN
STETTIN
BERLIN
ESSEN
DÜSSELDORF
COLOGNE
LEIPZIG
DRESDEN

GERMAN REPUBLIC

POSEN
THORN
BRESLAU
UPPER SILESIA

POLAND
BIALYSTOK
WARSAW
BREST LITOVSK
LODZ
LUTSK
KIEF

FRANCE
PARIS
VERDUN
Luxemburg
SAAR BASIN
LORRAINE
ALSACE
BELFORT
BASEL
BERNE
LYONS

SWITZERLAND
ULM
MUNICH
INNSBRÜCK
SOUTH TYROL

PRAGUE
PILSEN
BRNO
LINZ
VIENNA
BRATISLAVA

CZECHOSLOVAKIA

AUSTRIA
GRAZ

HUNGARY
BUDAPEST
DEBRECZEN
GROSSWARDEIN

CRACOW
PRZEMYSL
LVOV
Galicia
KAMENETS PODOLSK
CZERNOWITZ
BUKOVINA
Bessarabia

ROUMANIA
Transylvania
GALATZ

ITALY
MILAN
TURIN
GENOA
MONACO
MARSEILLES
TOULON

SLOVENIA
ZAGREB
ISTRIA
FIUME (IT. 1924)
VENICE
TRIESTE
CROATIA
ZARA (IT.)
BOSNIA
SARAJEVO
HERZE-GOVINA
SAN MARINO
FLORENCE
LAGOSTA (IT.)
MONTENEGRO

SLAVONIA
VOYVODINA
BELGRADE

JUGOSLAVIA
Serbia
NISH
SOFIA

BUCHAREST
PLOESTI
DOBRUJA
VARNA
BURGAS

BULGARIA

ALBANIA
DURAZZO
MONASTIR
MACEDONIA
SALONIKA

ADRIANOPLE
CONSTANTINOPLE
DEDEAGACH

Corsica (FR.)
ROME
NAPLES
BARI
TARANTO

Sardinia (ITAL.)

BIZERTA
TUNIS
PALERMO
Sicily
MESSINA

GREECE
ATHENS
CORINTH
SMYRNA
DODECANESE (ITAL.)

MALTA (BR.)
CRETE

To Greece 1920:
Recovered by
Turkey 1923.

44

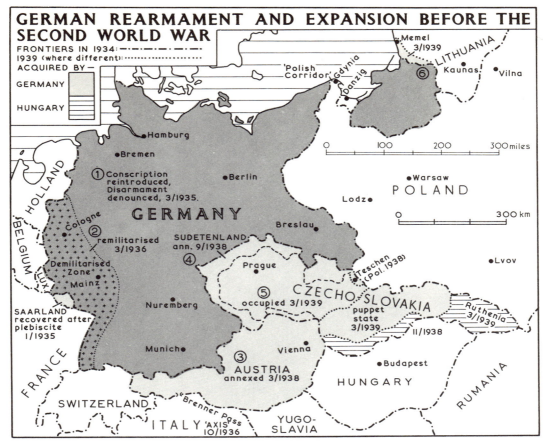

## GERMAN REARMAMENT AND EXPANSION BEFORE THE SECOND WORLD WAR

FRONTIERS IN 1934: ·-·-·-·-·-·
1939 (where different): ·-·-·-·-·-·
ACQUIRED BY —
GERMANY
HUNGARY

Memel 3/1939
LITHUANIA
Kaunas • Vilna
'Polish Corridor' • Gdynia
Danzig
⑥

0   100   200   300 miles

Hamburg •
Bremen •
① Conscription reintroduced, Disarmament denounced, 3/1935.
• Berlin
• Warsaw
POLAND
Lodz •

GERMANY
Breslau •

② remilitarised 3/1936
Cologne •
SUDETENLAND ann. 9/1938
④
Prague •
Teschen (Pol. 1938)
• Lvov

Demilitarised Zone
Mainz •
CZECHO-SLOVAKIA
⑤ occupied 3/1939
Ruthenia 3/1939

SAARLAND recovered after plebiscite 1/1935
Nuremberg •
puppet state 3/1939
11/1938

0   300 km

Munich •
Vienna •
• Budapest

③ AUSTRIA annexed 3/1938
HUNGARY
RUMANIA

FRANCE
SWITZERLAND
Brenner Pass
'AXIS 10/1936
ITALY
YUGO-SLAVIA

HOLLAND
BELGIUM
LUX.

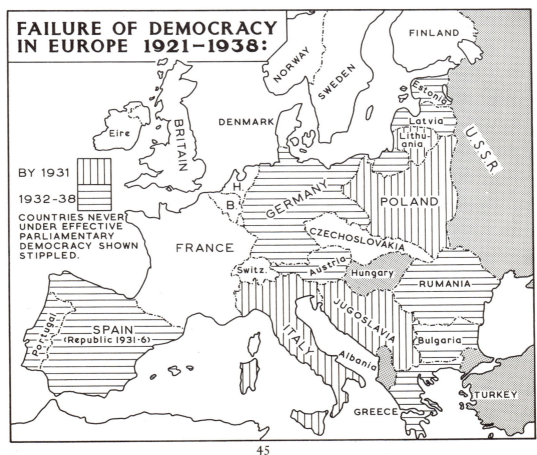

## FAILURE OF DEMOCRACY IN EUROPE 1921–1938:

BY 1931
1932-38
COUNTRIES NEVER UNDER EFFECTIVE PARLIAMENTARY DEMOCRACY SHOWN STIPPLED.

FINLAND
NORWAY
SWEDEN
Estonia
Latvia
Lithuania
USSR

Eire
BRITAIN
DENMARK
H.
B.
GERMANY
POLAND

FRANCE
CZECHOSLOVAKIA
Switz.
Austria
Hungary
RUMANIA
Portugal
SPAIN (Republic 1931-6)
ITALY
JUGOSLAVIA
Bulgaria
Albania
GREECE
TURKEY

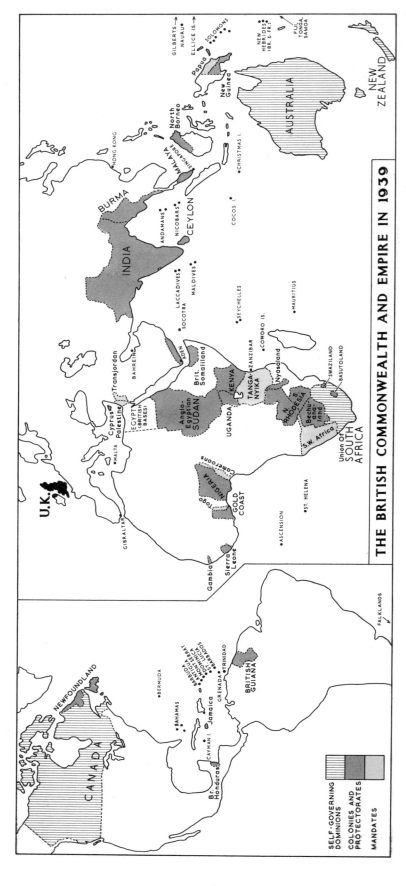

THE BRITISH COMMONWEALTH AND EMPIRE IN 1939

SELF-GOVERNING DOMINIONS

COLONIES AND PROTECTORATES

MANDATES

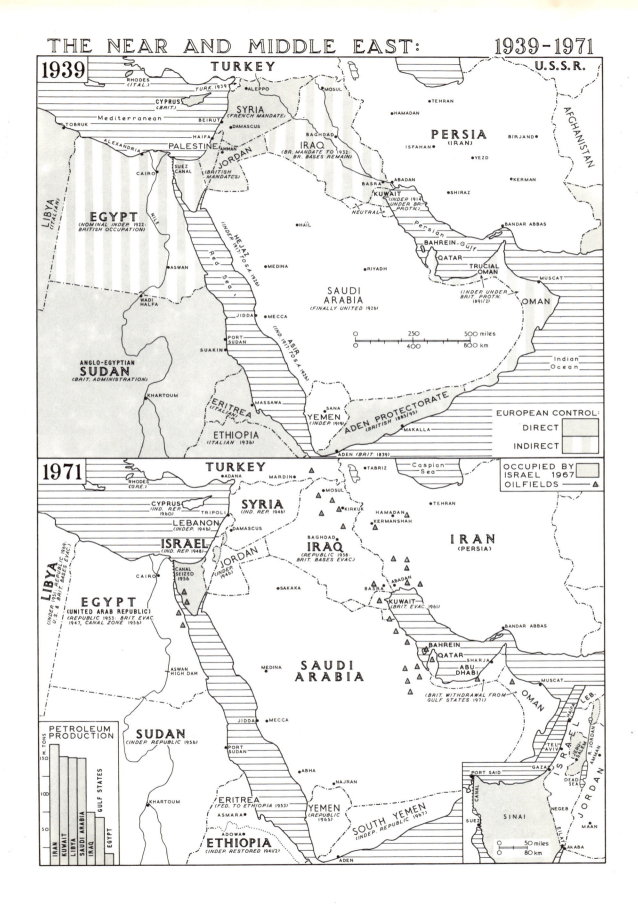

## 1939

TURKEY

U.S.S.R.

RHODES *(ITAL.)*
CYPRUS *(BRIT.)*
TURK. 1939
ALEPPO
MOSUL
SYRIA *(FRENCH MANDATE)*
TEHRAN
HAMADAN
PERSIA *(IRAN)*
BIRJAND
Mediterranean
TOBRUK
BEIRUT
DAMASCUS
BAGHDAD
ISFAHAN
HAIFA
AMMAN
PALESTINE
JORDAN
IRAQ *(BR. MANDATE TO 1932; BR. BASES REMAIN)*
YEZD
ALEXANDRIA
*(BRITISH MANDATES)*
CAIRO
SUEZ CANAL
BASRA
ABADAN
KERMAN
KUWAIT *(INDEP. 1914; UNDER BR. PROTN.)*
NEUTRAL
SHIRAZ
LIBYA *(ITALIAN)*
EGYPT *(NOMINAL INDEP. 1922; BRITISH OCCUPATION)*
NILE
HAÏL
Persian Gulf
BANDAR ABBAS
HEJAZ *(INDEP. TO S.A. 1926)*
Red Sea
BAHREIN *(BRIT.)*
QATAR
TRUCIAL OMAN
MUSCAT
ASWAN
RIYADH
*(INDEP. UNDER BRIT. PROTN. 1891/2)*
OMAN
WADI HALFA
MEDINA
SAUDI ARABIA *(FINALLY UNITED 1926)*
JIDDA
MECCA
ANGLO-EGYPTIAN SUDAN *(BRIT. ADMINISTRATION)*
PORT SUDAN
ASIR *(IND. 1917 TO S.A. 1926)*
250 / 500 miles
400 / 800 km
Indian Ocean
KHARTOUM
SUAKIN
MASSAWA
SANA
ERITREA *(ITALIAN)*
YEMEN *(INDEP. 1919)*
ADEN PROTECTORATE *(BRITISH 1885/95)*
MAKALLA
ETHIOPIA *(ITALIAN 1936)*
ADEN *(BRIT. 1839)*

EUROPEAN CONTROL:
DIRECT
INDIRECT

## 1971

TURKEY

Caspian Sea

OCCUPIED BY ISRAEL 1967
OILFIELDS ———▲

RHODES *(GRE.)*
ADANA
MARDIN
TABRIZ
CYPRUS *(IND. REP. 1960)*
TRIPOLI
SYRIA *(IND. REP. 1946)*
MOSUL
KIRKUK
HAMADAN
KERMANSHAH
TEHRAN
LEBANON *(INDEP. 1946)*
DAMASCUS
ISRAEL *(IND. REP. 1948)*
JORDAN *(INDEP. 1946)*
BAGHDAD
IRAQ *(REPUBLIC 1958; BRIT. BASES EVAC.)*
IRAN *(PERSIA)*
LIBYA *(INDEP. 1951; REPUBLIC 1969; U.S. & BRIT. BASES EVAC.)*
CAIRO
CANAL SEIZED 1956
SAKAKA
BASRA
ABADAN
EGYPT *(UNITED ARAB REPUBLIC)* *(REPUBLIC 1953; BRIT. EVAC. 1947, CANAL ZONE 1956)*
KUWAIT *(BRIT. EVAC. 1961)*
ASWAN HIGH DAM
MEDINA
BANDAR ABBAS
BAHREIN
QATAR
SHARJA
ABU DHABI
MUSCAT
SAUDI ARABIA
OMAN
*(BRIT. WITHDRAWAL FROM GULF STATES 1971)*
JIDDA
MECCA

PETROLEUM PRODUCTION
M. TONS
150
100
50
IRAN
KUWAIT
LIBYA
SAUDI ARABIA
IRAQ
EGYPT
GULF STATES

SUDAN *(INDEP. REPUBLIC 1956)*
PORT SUDAN
ABHA
NAJRAN
ERITREA *(FED. TO ETHIOPIA 1953)*
ASMARA
YEMEN *(REPUBLIC 1965)*
SOUTH YEMEN *(INDEP. REPUBLIC 1967)*
KHARTOUM
ADOWA
ETHIOPIA *(INDEP. RESTORED 1941/2)*
ADEN

PORT SAID
CANAL
SUEZ
SINAI
MALFA
TEL AVIV
JERUSALEM
GAZA
R. JORDAN
AMMAN
ISRAEL
LEB.
DEAD SEA
NEGEB
JORDAN
MAAN
EILAT
AKABA

50 miles
80 km

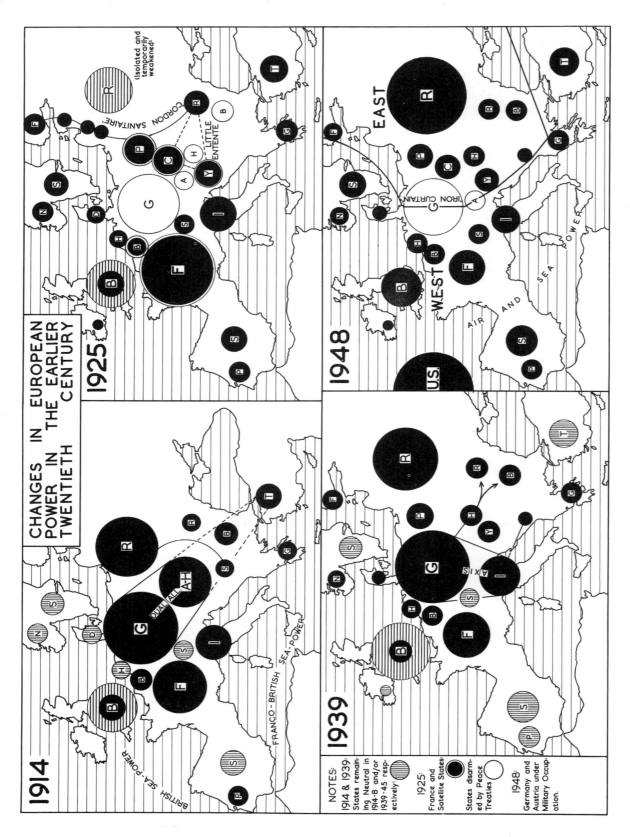

## CHANGES IN EUROPEAN POWER IN THE EARLIER TWENTIETH CENTURY

**1914**

BRITISH SEA-POWER

FRANCO-BRITISH SEA-POWER

DUAL ALL A·H

**1925**

CORDON SANITAIRE

LITTLE ENTENTE

(Isolated and temporarily weakened)

**1939**

AXIS

NOTES:
1914 & 1939: States remaining Neutral in 1914-8 and/or 1939-45 respectively:

1925: France and Satellite States:

States disarmed by Peace Treaties:

1948: Germany and Austria under Military Occupation.

**1948**

EAST

WEST

IRON CURTAIN

AIR AND SEA POWER

U.S.

The black circles are intended to give an approximate idea of the relative power of the different states and their groupings. Britain was the only Power of importance to have no peace-time conscription before 1939: the difference between her immediate and potential power is indicated by the horizontally shaded circle.

48

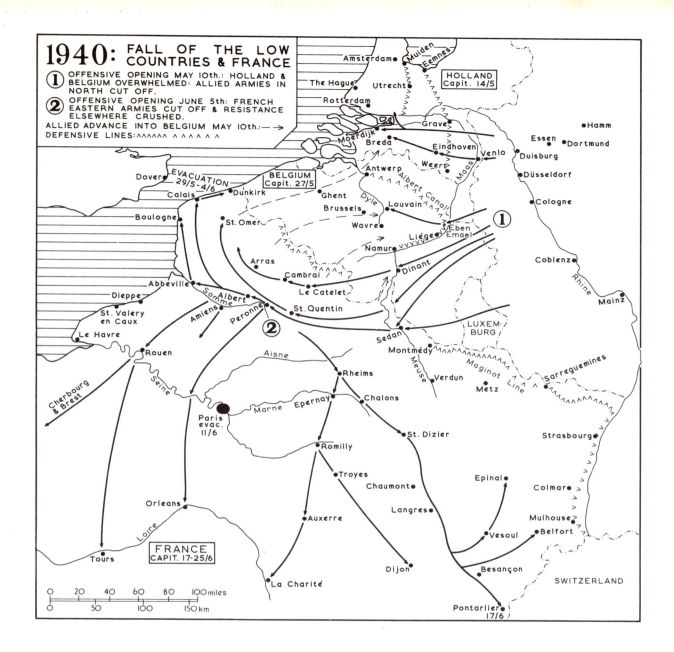

# 1940: FALL OF THE LOW COUNTRIES & FRANCE

① OFFENSIVE OPENING MAY 10th.: HOLLAND & BELGIUM OVERWHELMED: ALLIED ARMIES IN NORTH CUT OFF.

② OFFENSIVE OPENING JUNE 5th: FRENCH EASTERN ARMIES CUT OFF & RESISTANCE ELSEWHERE CRUSHED.

ALLIED ADVANCE INTO BELGIUM MAY 10th.:—→

DEFENSIVE LINES:∧∧∧∧∧∧ ∧ ∧ ∧ ∧ ∧ ∧

Amsterdam
Muiden
Eemnes
The Hague
Utrecht
Rotterdam
HOLLAND Capit. 14/5
Grave
Hamm
Essen
Dortmund
Breda
Eindhoven
Venlo
Duisburg
Weert
Maas
Düsseldorf
Moerdijk
Antwerp
Albert Canal
Cologne
Ghent
Dyle
Louvain
Dover
EVACUATION 29/5-4/6
Calais
Dunkirk
BELGIUM Capit. 27/5
Brussels
Wavre
Eben Emael
Boulogne
St. Omer
Liége
Coblenz
Namur
Arras
Dinant
Abbeville
Cambrai
Somme
Albert
Le Catelet
Rhine
Mainz
Dieppe
Peronne
St. Quentin
St. Valery en Caux
Amiens
Sedan
LUXEM-BURG
Le Havre
②
Montmédy
Maginot Line
Sarreguemines
Rouen
Aisne
Verdun
Meuse
Cherbourg & Brest
Seine
Rheims
Metz
Epernay
Chalons
Marne
Paris evac. 11/6
Romilly
St. Dizier
Strasbourg
Troyes
Chaumont
Epinal
Colmar
Orleans
Langres
Loire
Auxerre
Mulhouse
Belfort
Vesoul
Dijon
Besançon
Tours
FRANCE CAPIT. 17-25/6
La Charité
Pontarlier 17/6
SWITZERLAND

0  20  40  60  80  100 miles
0  50  100  150 km

49

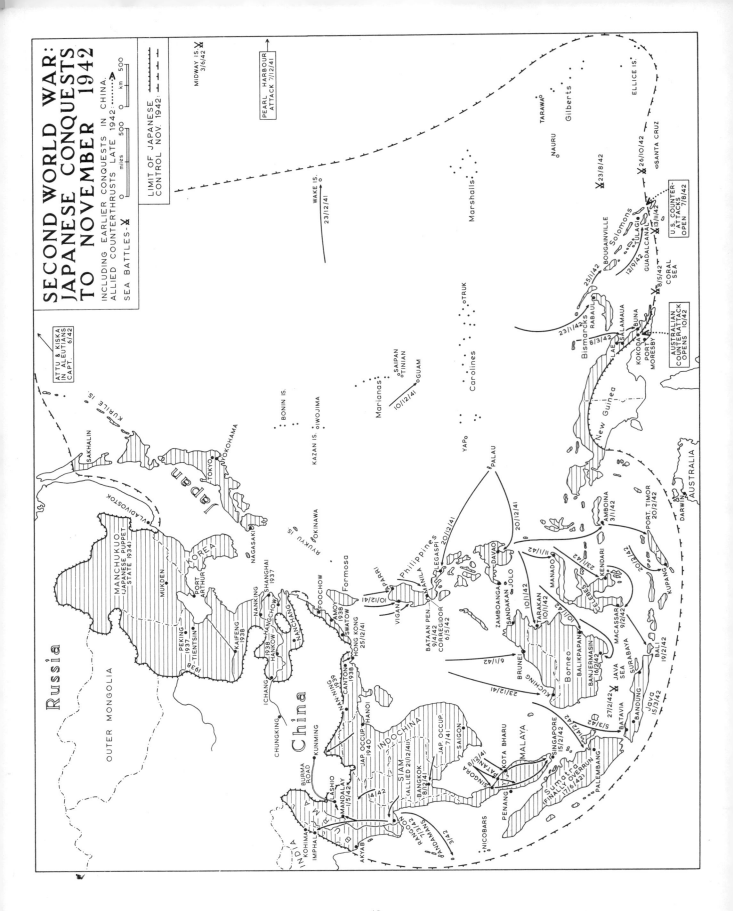

# SECOND WORLD WAR: JAPANESE CONQUESTS TO NOVEMBER 1942

INCLUDING EARLIER CONQUESTS IN CHINA.
ALLIED COUNTERTHRUSTS LATE 1942: ·········
SEA BATTLES - ✕

LIMIT OF JAPANESE
CONTROL NOV. 1942:

MIDWAY IS. ✕
3/6/42

PEARL HARBOUR
ATTACK 7/12/41

ATTU & KISKA
IN ALEUTIANS
CAPT. 6/42

km   500

miles   500

MARSHALLS

GILBERTS

ELLICE IS.

TARAWA

NAURU

SANTA CRUZ
✕ 26/10/42

U.S. COUNTER-
ATTACKS
OPEN 7/8/42

✕ 23/8/42

✕ 13/11/42

SOLOMONS
BOUGAINVILLE
TULAGI 12/9/42
GUADALCANAL

CORAL
SEA

AUSTRALIAN
COUNTER-ATTACK
OPENS 10/42

25/1/42

23/1/42 RABAUL
Bismarcks 8/3/42
LAE
SALAMAUA
BUNA
KOKODA
PORT
MORESBY

New Guinea

oTRUK

Carolines

YAPo

PALAU

SAIPAN
TINIAN
oGUAM
10/12/41

Marianas

KAZAN IS.
oIWOJIMA

BONIN IS.

WAKE IS. o
23/12/41

Russia

OUTER MONGOLIA

VLADIVOSTOK

SAKHALIN

KURILE IS.

Japan

TOKYO
oYOKOHAMA

NAGASAKI

MANCHUKUO
(JAPANESE PUPPET
STATE 1934)

KOREA

MUKDEN

PORT
ARTHUR

PEKING
1937
TIENTSIN 1938

KAIFENG
1938

NANKING

HANCHOW
1938
SHANGHAI
1937

NANCHANG

HANKOW
1938

ICHANG

China

CHUNGKING

KUNMING

NANNING 1939

CANTON
1938

HANOI

JAP OCCUP
1940

INDOCHINA

JAP OCCUP
7/41

SAIGON

SIAM
(ALLIED 21/12/41)

BANGKOK
8/12/41

BURMA
ROAD

LASHIO

MANDALAY
1/5/42

KOHIMA

IMPHAL

INDIA

AKYAB

ANDAMANS
23/3/42

RANGOON
7/3/42

NICOBARS

FOOCHOW

Formosa

AMOY
1938
SWATOW

HONG KONG
25/12/41

OKINAWA

RYUKYU IS.

VIGAN
10/12/41

Philippines

LEGASPI
12/12/41

MANILA

APARRI
10/12/41

BATAAN PEN.
9/4/42
CORREGIDOR
6/5/42

DAVAO
20/12/41

ZAMBOANGA
10/1/42
JOLO

SANDAKAN
19/1/42

ARAKAN
10/1/42

MANADO
11/1/42

KENDARI
23/1/42

Borneo

KUCHING
23/12/41

BRUNEI

BALIKPAPAN
16/2/42

BANJERMASIN
16/2/42

Celebes

MACASSAR
9/2/42

AMBOINA
3/1/42

PORT. TIMOR
20/2/42

KUPANG
20/2/42

Java
15/3/42

JAVA
SEA
27/2/42 ✕

SURABAYA

BALI
19/2/42

BANDUNG

BATAVIA

Sumatra
(FINALLY OVERRUN
17/6/42)

PALEMBANG

Malaya

SINGAPORE
15/2/42

PENANG

KOTA BHARU
8/12/41

KLANTANI
8/12/41

SINGORA

AUSTRALIA

DARWIN

PORT. TIMOR

6/1/42

28/1/42

11/1/42

20/12/41

50

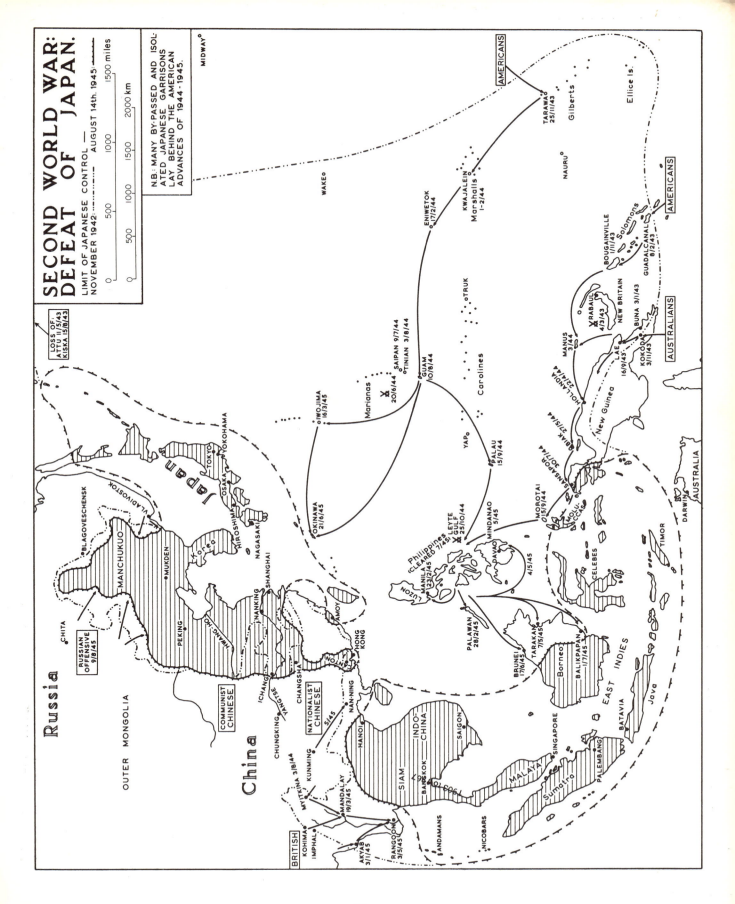

# SECOND WORLD WAR: DEFEAT OF JAPAN.

LIMIT OF JAPANESE CONTROL —
NOVEMBER 1942: · · · · AUGUST 14th. 1945: ───

| 0 | 500 | 1000 | 1500 miles |
| 0 | 500 | 1000 | 1500 | 2000 km |

N.B: MANY BY-PASSED AND ISOL-
ATED JAPANESE GARRISONS
LAY BEHIND THE AMERICAN
ADVANCES OF 1944-1945.

MIDWAY°

AMERICANS

TARAWA 25/11/43

Gilberts

Ellice Is.

WAKE°

NAURU°

KWAJALEIN
Marshalls
1-2/44

AMERICANS

ENIWETOK 17/2/44

°TRUK

Carolines

BOUGAINVILLE 1/11/43
Solomons

GUADALCANAL 8/2/43

RABAUL 4/3/43

NEW BRITAIN

BUNA 3/1/43

AUSTRALIANS

MANUS 3/44

LAE 16/9/43

KOKODA 3/11/43

SAIPAN 9/7/44
°TINIAN 3/8/44

GUAM 10/8/44

Marianas 20/6/44

°IWO JIMA 16/3/45

YAP°

PALAU 15/9/44

HOLLANDIA 22/4/44

BIAK 27/5/44

MOROTAI °15/9/44

New Guinea

DARWIN

AUSTRALIA

LOSS OF:
ATTU 11/5/43
KISKA 15/8/43

CHITA°

Russia

BLAGOVESCHENSK

VLADIVOSTOK

RUSSIAN OFFENSIVE 9/8/45

MANCHUKUO

MUKDEN°

PEKING°

OUTER MONGOLIA

Japan

TOKYO°
YOKOHAMA
OSAKA
HIROSHIMA
NAGASAKI

Korea

HWANG-HO

NANKING

SHANGHAI

China

ICHANG

YANGTSE

CHANGSHA

CHUNGKING

AMOY

HONG KONG

COMMUNIST CHINESE

NATIONALIST CHINESE 5/45

NAN-NING

KUNMING

HANOI°

MYITKINA 3/8/44

MANDALAY 19/3/45

INDO-CHINA

SAIGON

SIAM

BANGKOK

KOHIMA

IMPHAL

BRITISH

AKYAB 3/1/45

RANGOON 3/5/45

ANDAMANS

NICOBARS

MINDANAO 5/45

DAVAO

Philippines
CLEARED 7/45

LEYTE GULF 25/10/44

MANILA 23/2/45

LUZON

PALAWAN 28/2/45

MOLU-CCAS°

CELEBES

TIMOR

BRUNEI 17/6/45

TARAKAN 1/5/45

Borneo

BALIKPAPAN 1/7/45

EAST INDIES

Java

BATAVIA

SINGAPORE

MALAYA

PALEMBANG

Sumatra

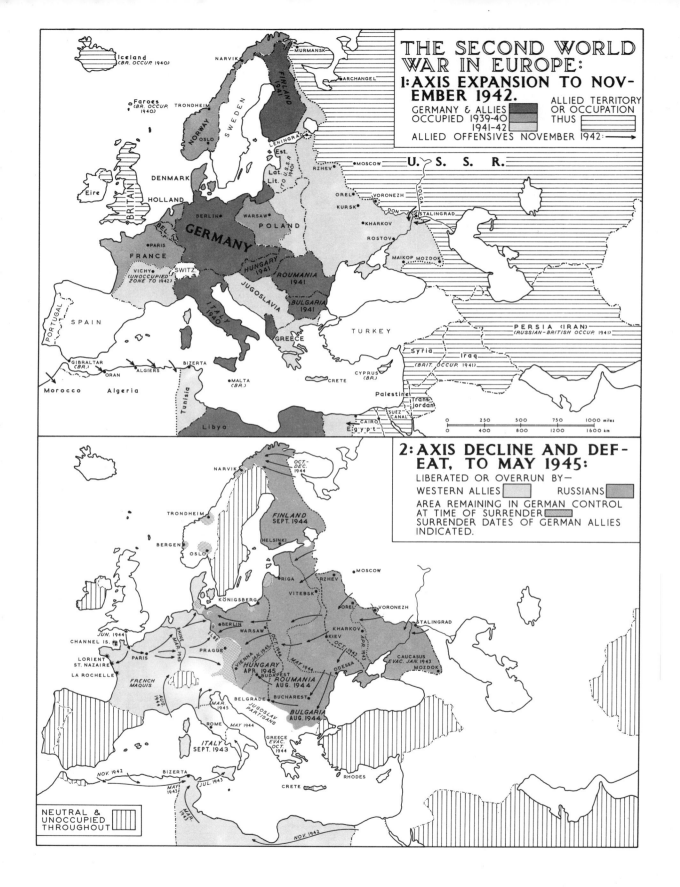

THE SECOND WORLD
WAR IN EUROPE:
1: AXIS EXPANSION TO NOV-
EMBER 1942.
GERMANY & ALLIES          ALLIED TERRITORY
OCCUPIED 1939-40          OR OCCUPATION
        1941-42          THUS
ALLIED OFFENSIVES NOVEMBER 1942:⟶

2: AXIS DECLINE AND DEF-
EAT, TO MAY 1945:
LIBERATED OR OVERRUN BY—
WESTERN ALLIES          RUSSIANS
AREA REMAINING IN GERMAN CONTROL
AT TIME OF SURRENDER
SURRENDER DATES OF GERMAN ALLIES
INDICATED.

NEUTRAL &
UNOCCUPIED
THROUGHOUT

INSET - Half Scale

NORWAY
SWEDEN
FINLAND
U.S.S.R.
Petsamo
Murmansk
Göteborg
Helsinki
Viborg
Porkkala
(Russ. 1945-56)
Leningrad

Stockholm
Gotland
Khiuma
Sarema
Leningrad
Novgorod
Tallinn
(ESTONIA)
Pskov
Libau
Riga
(LATVIA)
Klaipeda
(LITHUANIA)
Smolensk●
NETH.
DENMARK
SWEDEN
Copenhagen
Bornholm
(Dan.)
Gdansk
Kaliningrad
Kaunas
Vilna
Mogilev●
BELGIUM
Lübeck
Hamburg
Bremen
EAST GERMANY
BERLIN
(4 Power
control)
Szczecin
POLAND
Grodno
Minsk●
U.S.S.R.
Paris●
LUX.
Bonn
WEST GERMANY
Frankfort
Leipzig
Wroclaw
Warsaw
Lublin
Brest Litovsk
Chernigov●
Metz●
Strasbourg●
Prague
CZECHOSLOVAKIA
Cracow
Przemysl
Lvov
Kief●
FRANCE
Munich●
SWITZERLND.
Liechtenstein
Vienna
Bratislava
AUSTRIA
(NEUTRALISED)
Ruthenia
Chernovtsy
BESSARABIA
Lyons●
Budapest
HUNGARY
Jassy
Odessa●
Milan●
Trieste
Fiume
Zagreb
Belgrade
Arad
ROUMANIA
Marseilles●
Monaco●
San Marino
JUGOSLAVIA
(INDEPENDENT COMMUNIST STATE)
Sarajevo
Bucharest●
CORSICA
(Fr.)
ITALY
Rome●
Sofia
BULGARIA
SARDINIA
(Ital.)
Naples●
ALBANIA
Skoplje
Adrianople●
Tirana●
(COMMUNIST
REVOLT
SUPPRESSED)
Salonika
Istanbul
SICILY
Corfu
GREECE
TURKEY
Izmir●
Athens●
Dodecanese
(to Greece)
CRETE

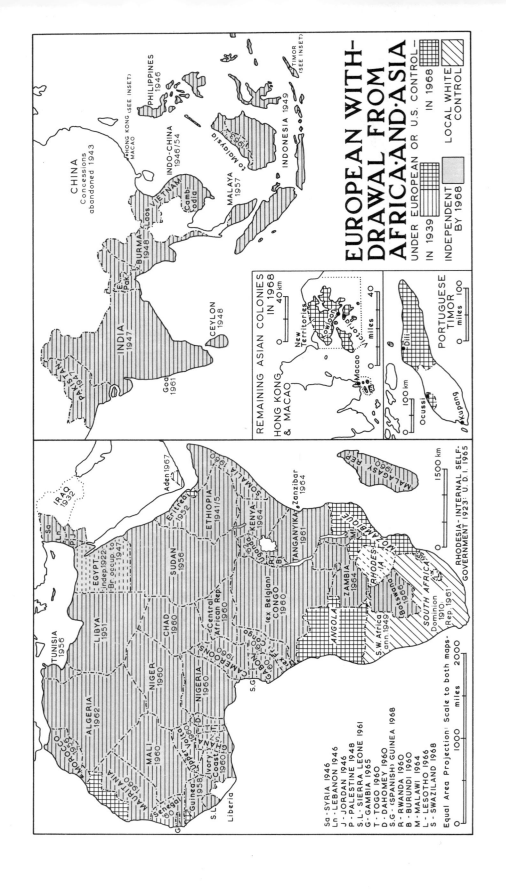

# EUROPEAN WITH-DRAWAL FROM AFRICA·AND·ASIA

UNDER EUROPEAN OR U.S. CONTROL—
IN 1939
IN 1968

LOCAL WHITE CONTROL

INDEPENDENT BY 1968

## Asia map (top)

CHINA
Concessions abandoned 1943

HONG KONG (SEE INSET)
MACAO

PHILIPPINES 1946

INDO-CHINA 1946/54

VIETNAM
Laos
Camb-odia

BURMA 1948

MALAYA 1957

INDONESIA 1949

SABAH 1963

TIMOR (SEE INSET)

INDIA 1947

PAKISTAN

E. Pak.

CEYLON 1948

Goa 1961

## REMAINING ASIAN COLONIES IN 1968

HONG KONG & MACAO

New Territories

KOWLOON
Victoria

Macao

miles 40
40 km

## PORTUGUESE TIMOR

Dili
Ocussi
Kupang

0 miles 100
0 100 km

## Africa map (bottom)

IRAQ 1932

Sa
Ln
P J

Aden 1967

EGYPT Indep.1922
Br. occup. to 1947

SUDAN 1956

ERITREA 1952

ETHIOPIA 1941/5

SOMALIA 1960

KENYA 1964

TANGANYIKA 1961

Zanzibar 1964

Uganda 1962

Central African Rep. 1960

CONGO (ex Belgian) 1960

RWANDA

BURUNDI

MALAGASY REP. 1960

TUNISIA 1956

LIBYA 1951

CHAD 1960

NIGER 1960

NIGERIA 1960

CAMEROONS 1960

GABON 1960

CONGO 1960

ANGOLA

ZAMBIA 1964

RHODESIA

MOZAMBIQUE

MALAWI

S.W. Africa ann. 1949
S. W. Africa

Botswana 1966

SOUTH AFRICA
Dominion 1910.
Rep. 1961

MOROCCO 1956

ALGERIA 1962

MALI 1960

MAURITANIA 1960

Senegal 1960

GUINEA 1958

Upper Volta 1960

Ivory Coast 1960

GHANA 1957

TOGO 1960

DAHOMEY 1960

S.L.
Liberia
G.
S.G.

LESOTHO

Sa - SYRIA 1946
Ln - LEBANON 1946
J - JORDAN 1946
P - PALESTINE 1948
S.L. - SIERRA LEONE 1961
G - GAMBIA 1965
T - TOGO 1960
D - DAHOMEY 1960
S.G. - (SPANISH) GUINEA 1968
R - RWANDA 1960
B - BURUNDI 1960
M - MALAWI 1964
L - LESOTHO 1966
S - SWAZILAND 1968

Equal Area Projection: Scale to both maps-

0   1000   2000
      miles

0   1500 km

RHODESIA- INTERNAL SELF-
GOVERNMENT 1923: U.D.I. 1965

54

INDIA: INDEPENDENCE AND PARTITION

PARTITION 1947: ——————
CEASE-FIRE LINE 1949: ················
FOREIGN ENCLAVES LATER
INCORPORATED UNDERLINED THUS:
FROM: FRANCE  PORTUGAL  OMAN

0 ————————— 500 miles
0 ————————— 800 km

Kabul

KASHMIR
Srinagar
JAMMU

AFGHANISTAN

Peshawar
Quetta

WEST PUNJAB
Lahore  Jullundur

PUNJAB  Simla
Patiala

Pakistan
INDEP. 1947: REPUB. 1956

BALUCHISTAN
BAHAWALPUR
Indus

Gwadar 1958

Karachi
SIND

RAJASTHAN

Delhi

UTTAR PRADESH

Jumna

Lucknow

TIBET
(Chinese Occup. 1950)

NEPAL

Lhasa

BHUTAN  ASSAM

Shillong
Imphal

EAST PAKI-STAN

MADHYA BHARAT

VINDHYA PRADESH

Bhopal

India
INDEP. 1947: REPUB. 1950

Rajkot

Diu 1961
Daman 1961
Bombay

BOMBAY

Nagpur

Rewah

MADHYA PRADESH

HYDERABAD 1949

Hyderabad

GOA 1961

INDIAN OCEAN

ANDHRA

Patna  Ganges

BIHAR

Chandernagore 1950
Calcutta

ORISSA

Cuttack

Yanaon 1954

BURMA
INDEP. REPUB. 1948

Irrawady
Rangoon

BAY OF BENGAL

Andaman Is.

MYSORE
Mercara

Madras

Laccadive Is.

Mahé 1954

Pondicherry
Karikal 1954

Bilaspur

Agartala

Nicobar Is.

To India

Trivandrum

Maldive Is.
(Brit. Prot.)

CEYLON
INDEP. 1948

Colombo

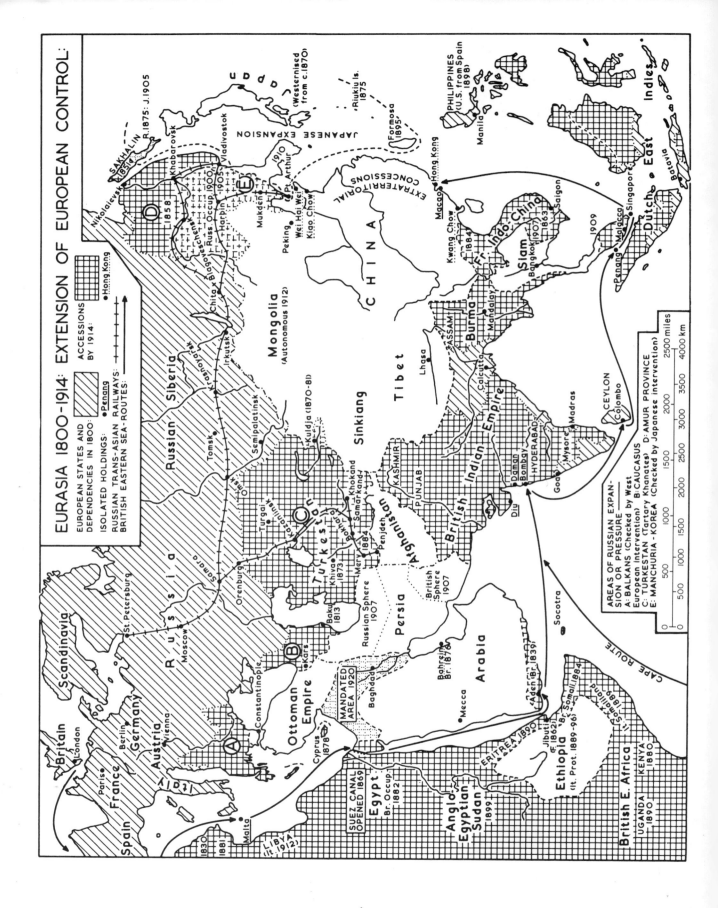

# EURASIA 1800-1914: EXTENSION OF EUROPEAN CONTROL:

EUROPEAN STATES AND
DEPENDENCIES IN 1800:

ISOLATED HOLDINGS: ● Penang

RUSSIAN TRANS-ASIAN RAILWAYS: +++++
BRITISH EASTERN SEA-ROUTES: ⟶

ACCESSIONS
BY 1914: +++++

● Hong Kong

**AREAS OF RUSSIAN EXPAN-
SION OR PRESSURE**
A: BALKANS (Checked by West
European intervention)   B: CAUCASUS
C: TURKESTAN (Tartary Khanates)   D: AMUR PROVINCE
E: MANCHURIA - KOREA (Checked by Japanese intervention)

Scale bars: 0 500 1000 1500 2000 2500 miles
0 500 1000 1500 2000 2500 3000 3500 4000 km

JAPAN (Westernised from c.1870)

Riukiu Is. 1875

Formosa 1895

JAPANESE EXPANSION

PHILIPPINES (U.S. from Spain 1898)

Manila

EXTRATERRITORIAL CONCESSIONS

Macao ● Hong Kong

East Indies

Dutch

Batavia

Singapore

Penang ● Malacca 1909

SAKHALIN 1850 R.1875: J.1905

Nikolaievsk

Khabarovsk

Vladivostok

Chita · Blagoveschensk · Russ. Occup. 1900

Harbin 1905

Pt. Arthur 1898

Mukden

Peking

Wei Hai Wei
Kiao Chow

Kwang Chow 1884

Fr. Indo-China

Saigon 1863

Bangkok (1907)

Siam

Mandalay

Burma

ASSAM

Calcutta

Colombo

CEYLON

D 1858

E 1910

Russian Siberia

Krasnoyarsk

Irkutsk

Tomsk

Semipalatinsk

Omsk

Kuldja (1870-81)

Mongolia (Autonomous 1912)

C H I N A

Tibet

Lhasa

Sinkiang

KASHMIR

PUNJAB

British Indian Empire

Mysore

Madras

HYDERABAD

Bombay

Goa

Daman

Diu

Turgai

Kazalinsk

Orenburg

Samara

Khiva 1873

Bokhara 1868

Merv 1884

Samarkand

Khokand

Penjdeh 1885

British Sphere 1907

Turkestan

Afghanistan

Persia

Russian Sphere 1907

Baku 1813

Kars

Mecca

Baghdad

MANDATED AREA 1920

Arabia

Bahrein Br. 1876

Mecca

Socotra

'Aden (Br. 1839)

ERITREA 1890

Jibuti (Fr. 1862)

Br. Somali. 1884

Ethiopia (It. Prot. 1889-96)

Somaliland 1889

British E. Africa

KENYA 1880

UGANDA 1890

Anglo-Egyptian Sudan 1899

Egypt Br. Occup. 1882

SUEZ CANAL OPENED 1869

Cyprus 1878

Constantinople

Ottoman Empire

A

B

Kars

Moscow

St. Petersburg

R u s s i a

Scandinavia

Britain London

France Paris

Spain

Portugal

Germany Berlin

Austria Vienna

ITALY

Malta

LIBYA (It. 1912)

1830

1881

CAPE ROUTE

# EURASIA

EGER
PO-
LAND
CZE.
HUN.
ROUM.
JUGOSL.
BULG.
AL.
(TO U.S.S.R.)
LENINGRAD

LENA
YAKUTSK

MOSCOW

U.  S.  S.  R.

OB

YENISEI

VLADIVOSTOK
MANCHURIA

VOLGA
TOBOLSK
STALINGRAD
OMSK
NOVOSIBIRSK
KRASNOYARSK
IRKUTSK
TANNU TUVA

SEMIPALATINSK

MONGOLIA
ULAN BATOR

N. KOREA
1945
S. KOREA

SAKHALIN

TURKEY

(1960)
(1948) (1946)
(1956) (1946)
IRAQ
(1932)
TEHRAN
IRAN
(PERSIA)
(1961)

TASHKENT

URUMCHI

PEKING

JAPAN

AFGHANISTAN

PAKISTAN
(1947)

(1971)

LADAKH

SINKIANG

TIBET
1950
LHASA

C H I N A

YENAN

NANKING

CHUNGKING
(CONCESSIONS
CEDED 1943)

U.S.-COMMUNIST
LINE OF
CONFRONTATION

FORMOSA (TAIWAN)
(NATIONALIST
CHINESE)

DELHI

KARACHI

(COMMUNIST CONTROL
COMPLETE 1949)
CANTON

HONG KONG
(BR.)

PHILIPPINES
(1946)

S. YEMEN
(1967)

INDIA
(1947)
(FR. SETTMTS. 1950-4:
PORT. 1961)
E. PAK-
ISTAN

BURMA
(1948)

LAOS

N. VIETNAM
1954

S. VIETNAM
(1949)

# COMMUNIST EXPANSION AND WESTERN WITHDRAWAL:
## AREA OF COMMUNIST CONTROL

1938                LATER EXPANSION

EXPANSIONIST PRESSURES·
DATES OF INDEPENDENCE AND/OR
WESTERN WITHDRAWAL IN BRACKETS.

CEYLON
(1948)

THAILAND
(SIAM)
CAMB-
ODIA

N. BORNEO
(1963)

MALAYA
(1957)

SINGAPORE

INDONESIA (1949)        (PORT.)

| 0 | 500 | 1000 | 1500 | 2000 miles |
|---|---|---|---|---|
| 0 | 800 | 1600 | 2400 | 3200 km |

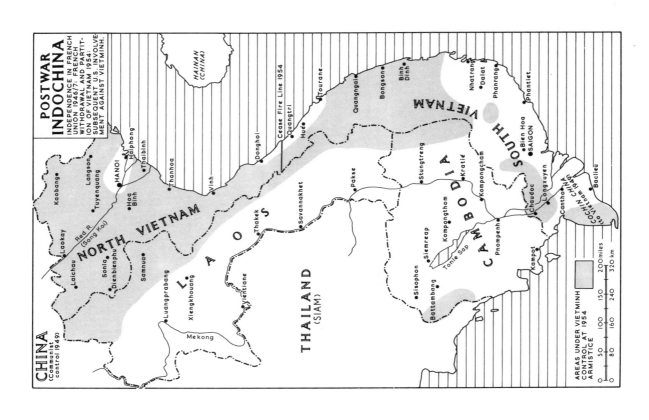

POSTWAR
INDOCHINA

INDEPENDENCE IN FRENCH
UNION 1946/7: FRENCH
WITHDRAWAL AND PARTIT-
ION OF VIETNAM 1954:
SUBSEQUENT U.S. INVOLVE-
MENT AGAINST VIETMINH.

CHINA
(Communist
control 1949)

HAINAN
(CHINA)

Cease Fire Line 1954

NORTH VIETNAM

Red R.
(Song Koi)

Kaobang
Langson
Tuyenquang
HANOI
Haiphong
Thaibinh
Thanhoa
Laokay
Laichau
Sonla
Dienbienphu
Samnua
Hoa
Binh
Vinh

L A O S

Luangprabang
Xiengkhouang
Vientiane
Thakek
Savannakhet
Pakse

Mekong

THAILAND
(SIAM)

Donghoi
Quangtri
Hué
Tourane

Quangngai
Bongson
Binh
Dinh
Nhatrang
Dalat
Phanrang
Phanthet

SOUTH VIETNAM

Stungtreng
Kratié
Kompongcham
Bien Hoa
SAIGON

Sisophon
Siemreap
Battambang
Kompongthom
Tonle Sap
Pnompenh
Kompot

C A M B O D I A

Chaudoc
Longxuyen
Cantho
COCHIN CHINA

COCHIN CHINA 1945

Baclieu

AREAS UNDER VIETMINH
CONTROL AT 1954
ARMISTICE

0  50  100  150  200 miles
0  80  160  240  320 km

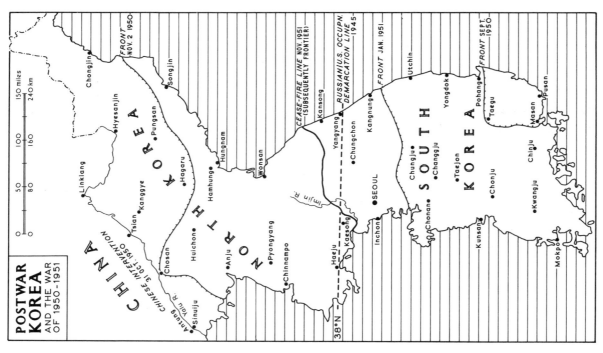

POSTWAR
KOREA
AND THE WAR
OF 1950-1951

0  50  100  150 miles
0  80  160  240 km

CHINA

Antung R.
Yalu R.
Sinuiju
CHINESE INTERVENTION 31 OCT. 1950
Chosan
Linkiang
Tsian
Kanggye
Huichon
Anju
Pyongyang
Chinnampo

N O R T H   K O R E A

Chongjin
Hyesanjin
Pungsan
Songjin
Hagaru
Hamhung
Hungnam
Wonsan

FRONT NOV. 2 1950

CEASE-FIRE LINE NOV.1951
(SUBSEQUENTLY FRONTIER)

Kansong
Yangyang
Chunchon
Kangnung

RUSSIAN/U.S. OCCUPN.
DEMARCATION LINE—1945

FRONT JAN. 1951

Utchin
Yongdok
Pohang

FRONT SEPT. 1950

Taegu
Pusan
Masan

S O U T H   K O R E A

Chungju
Changgju
Taejon
Chonju
Chitju
Kwangju

Imjin R.
Haeju
Kaesong
Inchon
SEOUL
Chonan

38°N

Kunsan
Mokpo

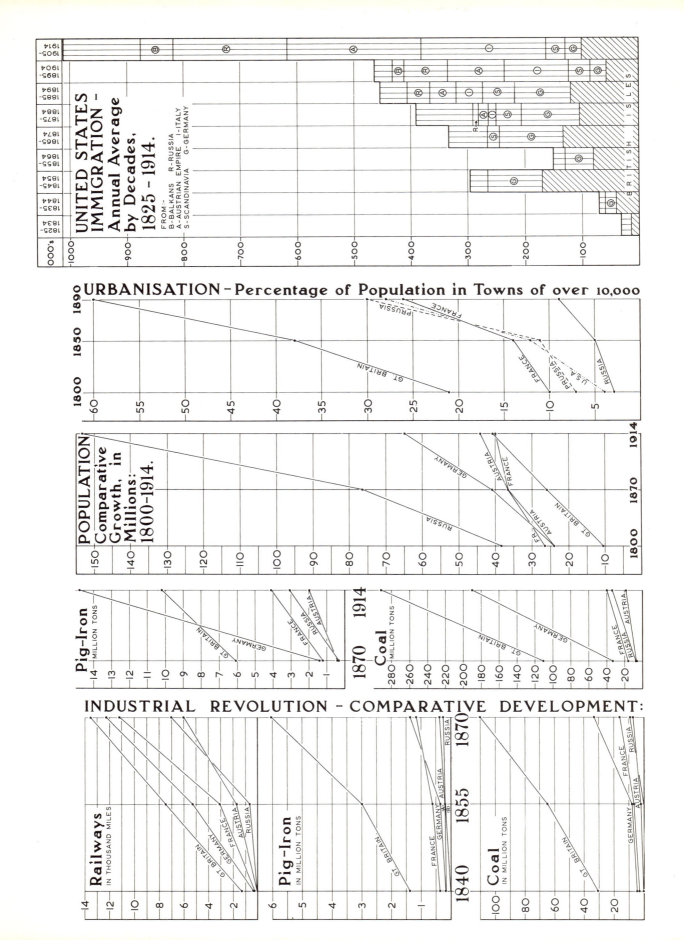

**UNITED STATES IMMIGRATION –** Annual Average by Decades, 1825 – 1914.

FROM:-
B–BALKANS  R–RUSSIA  I–ITALY
A–AUSTRIAN EMPIRE  G–GERMANY
S–SCANDINAVIA

'000's

BRITISH ISLES

**URBANISATION** – Percentage of Population in Towns of over 10,000

GT BRITAIN
PRUSSIA
FRANCE
U.S.A.
RUSSIA

**POPULATION** Comparative Growth, in Millions: 1800–1914.

RUSSIA
GERMANY
AUSTRIA
FRANCE
GT BRITAIN

**Pig-Iron** IN MILLION TONS

GT BRITAIN
GERMANY
FRANCE
RUSSIA
AUSTRIA

**Coal** IN MILLION TONS

GT BRITAIN
GERMANY
FRANCE
RUSSIA
AUSTRIA

**INDUSTRIAL REVOLUTION – COMPARATIVE DEVELOPMENT:**

**Railways** IN THOUSAND MILES

GT BRITAIN
GERMANY
FRANCE
AUSTRIA
RUSSIA

**Pig-Iron** IN MILLION TONS

GT BRITAIN
FRANCE
GERMANY
AUSTRIA
RUSSIA

**Coal** IN MILLION TONS

GT BRITAIN
GERMANY
AUSTRIA
FRANCE
RUSSIA

# INDEX

*(References are to page numbers, and for location only: each place has one reference, but may appear on several maps of the same area.)*

Chatham 22
Châtillon 17
Chattanooga 31
Chaudoc 58
Chaumont 17
Chefoo 38
Chelmsford 21
Cheltenham 23
Chernigov 53
Chester 21
Chesterfield 23
Cheyenne City 32
Chicago 30
Chichester 21
Chickamauga 31
Chilianwalah 37
Chinju 58
Chinkiang 38
Chinnampo 58
Chios 22
Chippenham 23
Chita 51
Chitral 37
Chonan 58
Chongjin 58
Chongju 58
Chosan 58
Christchurch (N.Z.) 34
Chungchon 58
Chungju 58
Chungking 38
Churchill 29
Cirencester 23
Ciudad Rodrigo 11
Civita Vecchia 19
Clearwater 32
Clermont 17
Clitheroe 22
Coblenz 9
Coburg 15
Cochin 36
Cochin-China 35
Cockermouth 23
Coeur d'Alene 32
Coimbra 11
Colchester 21
Cold Harbour 31
Colenso 27
Colesberg 27
Colmar 17
Cologne 9
Colombey 17
Colombo 36
Colorado Springs 32
Columbia 31
Columbus (Miss.) 31
Columbus (Tenn.) 31
Coni 8
Constantinople 14
Coolgardie 34
Copenhagen 12
Cordova 11
Corfe Castle 22
Corfu 10
Corinth 44
Corinth (U.S.) 31
Cormantine 27
Corunna 11
Cosenza 19
Coulmiers 17
Coupar Angus 23
Courcelles 17
Courtrai 13
Coventry 23
Cracow 12
Cranganore 36
Crazy Woman 32
Cremona 19
Crete 14
Crewe 23
Cricklade 21
Cripple Creek 32
Cristiansborg 27
Croydon 21
Culpeper 31
Curaçao 33
Custer 32

Custozza 19
Czernowitz 20

Dabo 37
Dacca 37
Dagö 5
Dahomey 27
Dalat 58
Dallas 32
Dalles, The 32
Daman 36
Damietta 28
Dansai 35
Danzig 44
Dardanelles 42
Dargai 37
Darlington 23
Darwin 34
Davao 50
Dawson City 29
De Aar 27
Deadwood 32
Deans Store 32
De Wets Dorp 27
Debreczen 20
Dedeagach 44
Dego 8
Delhi 36
Deming 32
Denbigh 22
Denison 32
Denver 32
Derby 23
Dermbach 16
Des Moines 30
Dessau 15
Detroit 30
Devizes 21
Devonport 22
Didcot 23
Dienbienphu 58
Dieppe 49
Dig 36
Dijon 49
Dili 54
Dilolo 28
Dinant 49
Dinapur 37
Dindings 35
Diu 36
Dobruja 22
Dodecanese 22
Dodge City 32
Dôle 17
Dominica 33
Doncaster 23
Donghoi 58
Dongola 28
Doornkop 26
Dorchester 23
Dorogobuzh 9
Dortmund 49
Dover 49
Downham 23
Downton 22
Dresden 16
Drissa 9
Droitwich 21
Drurys Bluff 31
Dublin 10
Dudley 21
Duem 37
Duisburg 49
Dulcigno 24
Dull Knife 32
Dum Dum 37
Dundee 23
Dundee (S. Af.) 27
Dunedin 34
Dunkirk 49
Dunwich 22
Durazzo 24
Durban 27
Durham 23
Düsseldorf 44
Dvinsk 44
Dybbøl 16

East Grinstead 22
East London 26
East Retford 22
Eboli 19
Eckmühl 9
Edinburgh 23
Edmonton 29
Eemnes 49
Eindhoven 49
Ekaterinburg 43
El Arish 28
El Obeid 28
El Paso 32
El Teb 28
Elandslaagte 27
Elba 10
Elk City 32
Ellice Is. 51
Ellsworth 32
Elmina 27
Elvas 11
Ely 23
Eniwetok 51
Enos 51
Epernay 17
Epinal 17
Epirus 24
Epsom 23
Erfurt 9
Erivan 43
Ermelo 27
Esmeralda 32
Essen 49
Eucla 34
Eupatoria 18
Eureka 32
Evesham 21
Evreux 17
Exeter 23
Eye 22
Eylau 9

Faizabad 37
Falkirk 21
Falkland Is. 46
Fargo 32
Farrukhabad 36
Fashoda 28
Fatehpur 37
Fauresmith 27
Fernandina 31
Fernando Po 25
Ferozepur 37
Ferozeshah 37
Ferrara 19
Ferrol 11
Fez 28
Figueras 11
Fiji 46
Finisterre 7
Fiume 44
Five Forks 31
Fleetwood 23
Flensburg 16
Fleurus 6
Flin Flon 29
Flint 22
Florence 19
Florence (U.S.) 32
Flores 35
Florina 24
Florisdorf 16
Flushing 13
Folkestone 23
Foochow 38
Forfar 23
Forli 19
Fort Apache 32
Fort Bayard 32
Fort Benton 32
Fort Bliss 32
Fort Bridger 32
Fort Buford 32
Fort Churchill 32
Fort Cobb 32
Fort Colville 32
Fort Donelson 31

Fort Ellis 32
Fort Fetterman 32
Fort Fisher 31
Fort Gibson 32
Fort Griffin 32
Fort Hall 32
Fort Henry 31
Fort Jackson 31
Fort James 27
Fort Kearney 32
Fort Klamath 32
Fort Laramie 32
Fort Lincoln 32
Fort McKinney 32
Fort McAllister 31
Fort Meade 32
Fort Monroe 31
Fort Morgan 31
Fort Nelson 29
Fort Peck 32
Fort Pillow 31
Fort Pulaski 31
Fort Randolph 31
Fort Reno 32
Fort Robinson 32
Fort Ross 32
Fort St David 36
Fort St John 29
Fort Sandeman 37
Fort Sill 32
Fort Smith 32
Fort Stanton 32
Fort Sumner 32
Fort Sumter 31
Fort Union 32
Fort Washakie 32
Fort Washita 32
Fort Wingate 32
Fort Worth 32
Fort Yuma 32
Fowey 22
Frankfort 9
Franklin (Can.) 29
Franklin (U.S.) 31
Fredericia 16
Fredericksburg 31
Frederiksborg 27
Freetown 27
Fremantle 34
Fribourg 13
Friedland 9
Friesland 13
Fuentes d'Onoro 11
Fulda 16
Funsbury 22
Fyn 16

Gaeta 19
Gainsborough 21
Galatz 44
Gallabat 28
Gallipoli 42
Galveston 30
Gatton 22
Gawilgarh 36
Gaza 42
Gdynia 45
Gelderland 13
Gembloux 11
Genappe 11
Geneva 13
Genoa 19
Geraldton 34
Gerona 11
Gettysburgh 31
Ghadames 28
Ghat 28
Ghazni 37
Ghent 13
Gheria 36
Gibraltar 7
Gilbert Is. 50
Gingi 36
Gisors 17
Gitschin 16
Gjatsk 9

Glamis 23
Glarus 13
Glasgow 21
Glastonbury 21
Glatz 16
Globe 32
Glogau 9
Gloucester 23
Glücksburg 16
Goa 36
Godalming 21
Gondokoro 28
Goole 21
Gold Creek 32
Goldsborough 31
Gorizia 20
Görz 20
Goshen 26
Gosport 23
Gotha 16
Gotland 5
Göteborg (Gothenburg)
    53
Goulburn 34
Graaf Reinet 26
Grahamstown 26
Grand Bassam 27
Grand Gulf 31
Grand Junction 31
Grantham 21
Graspan 27
Grave 49
Gravelotte 17
Gravesend 21
Graz 20
Great Bedwin 22
Great Driffield 21
Greenock 23
Greensborough 31
Greenwich 23
Grenada 33
Grenadines 33
Grimsby 22
Grisons 13
Grodno 9
Groningen 13
Groote Eylandt 34
Grossbeeren 9
Grossfriedrichsburg 27
Grosswardein 20
Guadalcanal 50
Guadeloupe 33
Guam 50
Guastalla 19
Guildford 21
Gujrat 37
Gwadar 55
Gwalior 37

Haarlem 13
Haderslev 16
Haeju 58
Hague, The 13
Haiderabad 37
Haifa 47
Haïl 47
Haiphong 58
Haiti 33
Hakodate 38
Halesworth 21
Halifax (Can.) 29
Halifax (Eng.) 22
Halmahera 35
Hamburg 9
Hameln 9
Hamhung 58
Hamm 49
Hanau 9
Hangchow 38
Hankow 38
Hanoi 58
Hanover 15
Harar 28
Harbin 14
Harpers Ferry 31
Harrisonburg 31
Harrogate 23

Hartlepool 23
Haslemere 22
Hastings 23
Hatteras 31
Havana 33
Heverfordwest 22
Hawkes Bay 34
Hay 21
Hayle 23
Hedon 22
Heilbron 27
Hejaz 47
Helder, The 13
Helena (Ark.) 31
Helena (Mont.) 32
Heligoland 12
Helsingford 12
Helsinki 44
Helston 22
Hereford 21
Herzegovina 20
Hesse 15
Heytesbury 22
Higham Ferrers 22
Hindon 22
Hiroshima 38
Hispaniola 33
Hoa Binh 58
Hobart 34
Hohenlinden 6
Hollandia 51
Holsworthy 21
Holstein 16
Hondschoote 6
Hong Kong 54
Honiton 22
Hooghly 36
Hoppstad 27
Horsham 22
Hougoumont 11
Houston 30
Huddersfield 23
Hudsons Bay 29
Hué 58
Hühnerwasser 16
Huichon 58
Hull 23
Humbold 32
Hungerford 23
Huntingdon 23
Husum 16
Hyderabad 36
Hyesanjin 58
Hythe 21

Ichang 38
Idaho City 32
Ifni 25
Iglau 16
Ilchester 22
Imbros 24
Imjin R. 58
Imphal 50
Indianapolis 30
Indore 37
Inkerman 18
Inn Viertel 20
Innsbrück 20
Inverurie 21
Ionial Is. 12
Ipswich 21
Irkutsh 14
Iron Gates 20
Isandhlwana 26
Isfahan 47
Isle of Pines 33
Ismailia 28
Istanbul 53
Istria 20
Iuka 31
Izmir 53

Jacatra 35
Jackson 31
Jaipur 36
Jalalabad 37
Jamaica 33

Janina 28
Jassy 12
Jemappes 6
Jena 9
Jhansi 37
Jhelum 37
Jibuti 28
Jidda 47
Johannesburg 27
Johnstone 21
Jokjakarta 35
Jolo 50
Jubbulpore 37
Jutland 16

Kabul 37
Kachar 37
Kaesong 58
Kaffa 28
Kaifeng 50
Kaiserslautern 17
Kalat 37
Kalgoorlie 34
Kalpi 37
Kaluga 9
Kamenets 44
Kamiesch 18
Kampot 58
Kandahar 37
Kandy 36
Kanggye 58
Kangnung 58
Kano 28
Kansas City 30
Kansong 58
Kaobang 58
Karachi 37
Karikal 36
Kars 43
Kassala 28
Kassel 16
Katmandu 37
Kaunas 53
Kavalla 24
Kazalinsk 14
Kazan 43
Kazatch Bay 18
Kearney 32
Keelung 38
Keewatin 29
Kem 43
Kendal 21
Kendari 50
Keighley 23
Kerch 18
Kerman 47
Keswick 23
Khabarovsk 14
Kharkov 43
Khartoum 28
Kherson 18
Khiva 14
Khokand 14
Kholapur 37
Khyber Pass 37
Kiaochow 38
Kidderminster 22
Kidwelly 21
Kiev 43
Kiel 16
Kilemba 28
Kimberley 27
Kinburn 18
King's Lynn 21
Kirbekan 28
Kirk Kilisse 24
Kirki 37
Kirkuk 47
Kissingen 16
Kiukiang 38
Kiungchow 38
Klagenfurt 20
Klaipeda 53
Klerksdorp 27
Klondike 29
Knaresborough 22
Knoxville 31

Kobe 38
Kodok 28
Kohima 50
Kokoda 50
Kolberg 9
Kolding 16
Kolombeng 28
Kolosvar 20
Komati Poort 27
Komorn 20
Kompongcham 58
Kompongthom 58
Konakri 27
Kong 28
Königgrätz 16
Königsberg 9
Kordofan 28
Kororarika 34
Korti 28
Kosseir 28
Kota Bharu 50
Köthen 15
Kotlas 43
Kovno 9
Kowloon 54
Krasnoi 9
Krasnoyarsk 57
Krat 35
Kratié 58
Kronstadt 43
Kroonstad 27
Kuching 50
Kufra 28
Kuka 28
Kukawa 28
Kuldja 14
Kumanovo 24
Kumasi 27
Kunming 50
Kunsan 58
Kupang 50
Kurile Is. 50
Kursk 52
Kuruman 28
Küstrin 9
Kut el Amara 42
Kuwait 47
Kwajalein 51
Kwangchow 38
Kwangju 58

La Fère 9
La Rochelle 52
Labuan 35
Laccadive Is. 55
Ladysmith 27
Lae 50
Lagos 27
Lagosta 44
Lahore 37
Laichau 58
Lancaster 21
Landau 17
Landrecies 17
Landshut 9
Langensalza 16
Langres 17
Langson 58
Laokay 58
Laon 17
Laramie 32
Lashio 50
Las Vegas 32
Laswari 36
Lauenburg 16
Laufach 16
Launceston 21
Launceston (Tas.) 34
Le Havre 17
Leadville 32
Lebanon 47
Lechlade 21
Leeds 21
Leeward Is. 33
Legaspi 50
Leghorn 19
Legnago 19

Leicester 23
Leipzig 16
Lemberg (Lvov) 20
Lemnos 24
Leningrad 44
Leominster 21
Lerida 11
Lewes 21
Lexington (Miss.) 31
Leyte 51
Lhasa 37
Libau 44
Lichfield 21
Lichtenburg 27
Liechtenstein 15
Liége 15
Ligny 11
Lille 17
Limburg 13
Lincoln 23
Lindfield 21
Lindley 27
Linkiang 58
Linz 9
Lipari Is. 19
Lisbon 11
Liskeard 21
Lissa 10
Little Big Horn 32
Liverpool 21
Loanda 25
Loano 8
Lodi 8
Lodz 44
Lombok 35
Lonato 8
London 10
Longwy 17
Longxuyen 58
Looe 21
Lorenco Marques 26
Lorient 52
Los Angeles 30
Lostwithiel 22
Louisville 31
Louth 21
Louvain 13
Lowestoft 21
Luangprabang 58
Lübeck 9
Lublin 45
Lucca 19
Lucerne 13
Lucknow 36
Ludgershall 22
Ludlow 22
Lule Burgas 24
Lunéville 17
Lutsk 44
Luxemburg 13
Luzon 35
Lvov 44
Lydenburg 27
Lymington 22
Lyons 6
Lytham 23

Maastricht 13
Macao 54
Macassar 35
Macclesfield 22
Macedonia 24
Machadodorp 27
Mackenzie (Can.) 29
Mackenzie (U.S.) 32
Macon 31
Maddalena Bay 7
Madras 36
Madrid 11
Madura 35
Mafeking 27
Magdala 28
Magdeburg 9
Magenta 19
Magersfontein 27
Mahé 36

Maidenhead 23
Maidstone 23
Maikop 52
Mainz 9
Majuba 26
Makale 28
Makalla 47
Malacca 35
Malaga 11
Maldive Is. 55
Malmédy 44
Malmesbury 22
Malo Jaroslavetz 9
Malta 10
Malton 22
Manado 50
Manassas 31
Manchester 23
Mandalay 50
Mangalore 36
Manila 35
Manipur 37
Mannheim 9
Mantua 8
Manus 51
March 21
Marengo 6
Margate 23
Mariana Is. 51
Marie Galante 33
Marietta 31
Market Weighton 21
Marlborough 22
Marsal 17
Marsala 19
Marseilles 6
Marshall Is. 50
Martinique 33
Maryport 23
Marysville 32
Masan 58
Massa 19
Massawa 28
Masulipatam 36
Maubeuge 17
Mauritius 46
Mazovia 8
Mecca 28
Mecklenburg 15
Medina 28
Meerut 37
Melbourne 34
Melito 19
Melton 23
Memel 44
Mentana 19
Meran 40
Mercara 55
Meridian 31
Merthyr Tydvil 22
Merv 14
Messina 19
Metemma 28
Metx 6
Métzières 17
Miani 37
Middelburg (S. Af.) 27
Middlesbrough 23
Midhurst 21
Midia 24
Midway Is. 50
Milan 8
Milazzo 19
Milbourne Port 22
Mildenhall 21
Miles City 32
Mill Spring 31
Milledgeville 31
Milwaukee 30
Mindanao 35
Minehead 22
Minneapolis 30
Minorca 6
Minsk 9
Miquelon 29
Miskolcz 20
Missionary Ridge 31

Missoula 32
Mitylene 24
Mobile 31
Modder R. 27
Modena 19
Moerdijk 49
Mojaisk 9
Mokpo 38
Moldavia 12
Moluccas 35
Monaco 12
Monastir 24
Mondovi 8
Monmouth 21
Monrovia 27
Mons 13
Montbard 17
Montebello 19
Montenegro 24
Montenotte 8
Monterey 32
Montgomery 22
Montgomery (U.S.) 31
Montmédy 17
Montreal 29
Montserrat 33
Moravia 20
Morpeth 22
Morotai 51
Moscow 9
Mosquito Coast 33
Mossel Bay 26
Mostar 20
Mosul 47
Motherwell 23
Mountain Pass 32
Mount Morgan 34
Mozdok 54
Mühlhausen 10
Mulhouse 17
Multan 37
Münchengrätz 16
Munich 16
Munkacz 20
Murfreesboro 31
Murmansk 43
Miroran 38
Murzuk 28
Muscat 47
Mytho 35

Naauport 27
Nachod 16
Nagasaki 38
Nagpur 37
Namur 13
Nanking 38
Nanning 50
Nantes 6
Nantwich 21
Napier 34
Naples 19
Narborough 23
Narvik 52
Nashville 31
Nasirabad 37
Nauru 50
Navarino 14
Neerwinden 6
Negapatam 36
Neilston 23
Nelson (N.Z.) 34
Nessib 14
Neu Breisach 17
Neuchatel 13
Neufchâteau 17
Nevada City 32
Nevers 17
Nevis 33
New Brunswick 29
New Madrid 31
New Malton 21
New Orleans 31
New Plymouth 34
New Romney 22
New York 30
Newark 21

Newbury 23
Newcastle (Aust.) 34
Newcastle-on-Tyne 23
Newcastle-under-Lyme 22
Newchwang 38
Newhaven 21
Newport (Corn.) 22
Newport (I.O.W.) 22
Newport (Mon.) 23
Newport Pagnell 21
Newton (Lancs.) 22
Newton (U.S.) 32
Newton Abbot 23
Newtown (I.O.W.) 22
Newtown (Salop) 21
Nhatrang 58
Nice 17
Nicobar Is. 51
Niigata 38
Nijmegen 13
Nikolaievsk 14
Nikolsburg 16
Ningpo 38
Nich 24
Noisseville 17
Nooitgedacht 27
Norman Wells 29
North Shields 23
North Walsham 21
Northallerton 22
Northampton 21
Norwich 21
Nottingham 21
Nova Scotia 29
Novara 19
Novgorod 53
Novibazar 20
Novosibirsk 57
Nuits 17
Nürnberg 16
Nyangwe 28
Nylstrom 27

Oakham 21
Oakland 32
Obok 28
Ocussi 54
Odense 16
Odessa 52
Ogaden 28
Ogallala 32
Ogden 32
Okehampton 22
Okinawa 50
Old Providence 33
Old Sarum 22
Oldenburg 15
Olmütz 16
Omaha 30
Oman 47
Omdurman 28
Omsk 14
Oodnadatta 34
Oporto 11
Oran 52
Orbetello 19
Oregon City 32
Orel 52
Orenburg 14
Orford 22
Orissa 37
Orleans 17
Orofino 32
Orsha 9
Orsova 20
Orthez 11
Oruba 33
Osaka 38
Ösel 35
Oslo 44
Ostend 13
Otago 34
Otaru 38
Ottawa 29
Oxford 21

Paardeberg 27
Padang 35
Padua 19
Paducah 31
Paisley 23
Pakhoi 38
Pakse 58
Palau 51
Palawan 35
Palembang 35
Palermo 19
Palestra 19
Pamplona 11
Panay 35
Paniput 36
Papelotte 11
Paramatta 34
Pardubitz 16
Paris 17
Parma 19
Patani 50
Patay 17
Patna 36
Pavia 19
Pecs 20
Peking 38
Pembrey 21
Pembroke 22
Penang 35
Penjdeh 14
Penrith 23
Penryn 22
Pensacola 31
Perekop 18
Perim 28
Perm 43
Péronne 17
Perpignan 6
Perryville 31
Perth (Aust.) 34
Perth (Scot.) 23
Pesciera 19
Peshawar 37
Peterborough 21
Petersburg (Va.) 31
Petersfield 22
Peterwardein 20
Petrograd 43
Phanrang 58
Phantiet 58
Phantom Hill 32
Philadelphia 31
Philippine Is. 50
Phoenix 32
Piacenza 19
Pickering 23
Pierce 32
Pietermaritzburg 27
Pietersburg 27
Piquetberg 26
Pisa 19
Pittsburg 31
Placerville (Cal.) 32
Placerville (Idaho) 32
Plancenoit 11
Plassey 36
Plevna 24
Ploesti 20
Plymouth 7
Plympton 22
Pnompenh 58
Podlesia 8
Podolia 8
Pohang 58
Pola 20
Pomerania 44
Pondicherry 36
Pont à Mousson 17
Pontarlier 17
Pontecorvo 19
Pontypool 23
Poona 36
Port Arthur (Can.) 29
Port Arthur (China) 38
Port au Prince 33
Port Augusta 34
Port Elizabeth 26

Port Essington 34
Port Hudson 31
Port Jackson 34
Port Macquarie 34
Port Moresby 50
Port Nelson 29
Port of Spain 33
Port Philip 34
Port Radium 29
Port Said 28
Port Sudan 28
Portland (U.S.) 30
Portobello 33
Porto Novo 36
Porto Rico 33
Porto Seguro 27
Portsmouth 23
Posen 9
Potchefstrom 26
Prague 19
Prescott 32
Pressburg 20
Preston 23
Pretoria 27
Prince Edward I. 29
Prince George 29
Prince Rupert 29
Provins 17
Przemysl 20
Pskov 44
Pulicat 36
Pulo Condore 35
Pulo Run 35
Pungsan 58
Punniar 37
Pusan 58
Pyongyang 58

Quangngai 58
Quangtri 58
Quatre Bras 11
Quebec 17
Queenborough 22
Quelimane 28
Quetta 37
Quiberon 6
Quilon 36

Rabaul 50
Radnor 22
Ragusa 5
Raleigh 31
Rampur 36
Rampura 36
Ramsey 21
Ramsgate 23
Rangoon 50
Rankin Inlet 29
Ravenna 19
Rawalpindi 37
Reading 21
Red Lake 29
Redruth 23
Regensburg 9
Reggio 19
Regina 29
Reigate 22
Resaca 31
Rethel 17
Reuss 15
Reval 12
Rewah 55
Rheims 17
Rhodes 52
Rhondda 23
Ribe 19
Rich Mtn. 31
Richmond (Yorks.) 22
Richmond (Va.) 31
Rieti 19
Riga 12
Ripon 21
Riyadh 47
Rochdale 21
Rochefort 7
Rochester 21
Rockhampton 34

Rocroi 17
Rohilkand 36
Romagna 19
Rome 6
Romford 23
Romilly 49
Roseburg 32
Rostov 52
Rotherham 23
Rotterdam 13
Rouen 17
Ruabon 23
Rugby 23
Russel 34
Rustenburg 27
Rye 21
Rzhev 52

Saar Basin 44
Saarbrücken 17
Saareguemines 49
Saarwerden 6
Saba 35
Sadowa 16
Sahagun 11
Saigon 35
St Andrew (W.I.) 33
St Bartholomew 33
St Cloud 17
St Columb 21
St Eustatius 33
St Gallen 13
St George's Cay 33
St Germans 22
St Helena 46
St Ives 22
St John (Can.) 29
St John (W.I.) 33
St Johns 29
St Kitts 33
St Lucia 33
St Martin 33
St Mawes 22
St Michael 22
St Nazaire 52
St Omer 49
St Paul 30
St Petersburg 12
St Quentin 17
St Thomas 33
St Valery en Caux 49
St Vincent 33
St Vincent, Cape 7
Saipan 51
Sakaka 47
Sakhalin 38
Salamanca 11
Salamaua 50
Salerno 19
Salisbury 23
Salm 6
Salmon City 32
Salonica 42
Salsette I. 36
Salt Lake City 30
Saltash 22
Saltburn 23
Salzburg 20
Samar 35
Samarkand 14
Samnua 58
Samos 24
San Antonio 32
San Diego 32
San Domingo 33
San Francisco 30
San Juan de Ulua 33
San Marino 19
San Sebastian 11
Sana 47
Sandakan 50
Sand Creek 32
Sandwich 21
Sansapor 51
Santa Barbara 32
Santa Cruz (W.I.) 33
Santa Fe 30

Santander 11
Santiago (Cuba) 33
Saragossa 11
Sarajevo 20
Sarawak 35
Sarrebourg 17
Saskatoon 29
Savannakhet 58
Saverne 17
Savona 8
Savoy 6
Scarborough 23
Schaffhausen 13
Schässburg 20
Schefferville 29
Schwechat 20
Schwytz 13
Scutari (Albania) 24
Seattle 30
Sebastopol 18
Sedan 17
Segesvar 20
Selby 23
Semipalatinsk 14
Senafe 28
Senegal 27
Sennar 28
Seoul 38
Serampur 36
Seringapatam 36
Seville 11
Seychelles 46
Shaftesbury 22
Shanghai 38
Shashi 38
Sheffield 23
Shendi 28
Shenkursk 43
Shillong 55
Shiloh 31
Shimoda 38
Shimonoseki 38
Shoa 28
Shoreham 21
Shrewsbury 21
Siemreap 58
Siena 19
Sikkim 37
Silistria 24
Silver City 32
Silver Creek 32
Simbirsk 43
Simferopol 18
Simla 37
Singapore 35
Singora 50
Sinkiang 57
Sinope 14
Sinuiju 58
Sisophon 58
Siwa 28
Skipton 23
Sleaford 21
Smolensk 9
Smyrna 44
Sobraon 37
Socotra 56
Soda Springs 32
Sofia 24
Soissons 17
Sokoto 28
Solferino 19
Solomon Is. 51
Solothurn 13
Sonderborg 16
Songjin 58
Sonla 58
Sonora 32
Southampton 23
South Mount 32
South Pass 32
Southwark 22
Speyer 6
Spezia 19
Spicheren 17
Spion Kop 27

Spokane 32
Srinagar 37
Stafford 21
Stamford 23
Stabderton 27
Stellaland 26
Stellenbosch 26
Stettin 9
Steyning 22
Stockach 6
Stockbridge 21
Stockholm 10
Stockport 21
Stockton (Eng.) 23
Stockton (U.S.) 32
Stoke (on Trent) 21
Stoke Ferry 21
Stormberg 27
Stourport 21
Stowmarket 21
Straits Settlements 35
Stralsund 9
Strasbourg 49
Strasbourg (U.S.) 31
Stratford on Avon 21
Strelitz 15
Stroud 21
Stuhlweissenburg 20
Stungtreng 58
Stuttgart 16
Styria 20
Suakin 28
Sudbury 21
Sudetenland 45
Suez 28
Sula 35
Sumatra 35
Sumbawa 35
Sunderland 23
Surabaya 50
Surat 36
Sveaborg 5
Svendborg 16
Swansea 21
Swatow 38
Swaziland 26
Swellendam 26
Swindon 23
Sydney 34
Syracuse 19
Szeged 20
Szekesfehervar 20
Szöreg 20

Tabora 28
Tabriz 47
Tacna 33
Tacoma 32
Taegu 58
Taejon 58
Takao 38
Tallinn 44
Tamai 28
Tamworth 23
Tangier 25
Tanjore 36
Tannenberg 42
Taormina 19
Taos 32
Tarakan 50
Taranaki 34
Tarawa 50
Tarnopol 20
Tarragona 11
Tascosa 32
Tashkent 14
Taunton 21
Tauranga 34
Tavistock 21
Tchernaya 18
Teano 19
Tehran 47
Teignmouth 23
Telegraph Creek 29
Tel el Kebir 28

Temesvar 20
Tenbury 21
Ternate 35
Terni 19
Teschen 45
Tewkesbury 22
Thabanchu 26
Thaibinh 58
Thakek 58
Thanhoa 58
Theodosia 18
Thetford 23
Thionville 17
Thorn 8
Thouars 6
Thurgau 13
Tidor 35
Tientsin 38
Tiflis 43
Tigre 28
Tilsit 9
Timbuctu 28
Timor 35
Tinian 51
Tiverton 22
Tobago 33
Tobolsk 57
Todi 19
Tokar 28
Tokio 38
Toledo 11
Tombstone 32
Tomsk 14
Tonbridge 21
Tongue 32
Topeka 32
Toronto 29
Torres Vedras 11
Torrington 21
Tortosa 11
Tortuga 33
Toski 28
Totnes 23
Toul 17
Toulon 6
Toulouse 11
Tourane 58
Tourcoing 6
Townsville 34
Trafalgar 7
Tranquebar 36
Transylvania 20
Trapani 19
Trebbia 6
Tregony 22
Trichinopoli 36
Trier 6
Trieste 8
Trincomali 36
Tring 23
Trinidad 33
Tripoli 28
Trivandrum 55
Trondheim 54
Troyes 49
Truk 51
Truro 22
Tsaritsin 43
Tsian 58
Tsushima 38
Tucson 32
Tugela R. 27
Tula 9
Tulagi 50
Tulbagh 26
Tungchow 38
Turin 19
Turks Is. 33
Tuyenquang 58
Tyrol 19

Udaipur 37
Ufa 43
Ujiji 28
Ulan Bator 57

Ulm 9
Ulundi 26
Umbria 19
Ungava 29
Unterwalden 13
Uranium City 29
Uri 13
Urumchi 57
Ushant 7
Utchin 58
Utrecht 13
Utrecht (S. Af.) 26
Uttoxeter 21

Valencia 11
Valenciennes 17
Valladolid 11
Valmy 6
Vancouver 29
Varna 14
Vaud 13
Vellore 37
Vendée, La 6
Venice 19
Venlo 13
Verdun 17
Vereeniging 27
Verona 19
Versailles 17
Vesoul 17
Vichy 54
Vicksburg 31
Victoria (Can.) 29
Victoria I. 29
Vienna 14
Vientiane 58
Vigan 50
Vilagos 20
Villersexel 17
Vilna 44
Vimiero 11
Vincennes 17
Vinh 58
Vionville 17
Virginia (Mont.) 32
Virginia City 32
Virgin Is. 33
Vitebsk 52
Vittoria 11
Vladikavkaz 43
Vladivostok 38
Volhynia 8
Volkovisk 9
Vologda 43
Volokolamsk 9
Volterra 19
Volturno 19
Voronezh 52
Voyvodina 20
Vryburg 27
Vryheid 26
Vyatka 43

Wadebridge 23
Wadi Halfa 28
Wagadugu 28
Wagon Box 32
Wagram 9
Waikato 34
Waitangi 34
Waitara 34
Wake I. 51
Walcheren 13
Wallachia 14
Walla Walla 32
Wallingford 22
Walsall 22
Walvis Bay 25
Wandewash 36
Wanganui 34
Wantage 21
War Bonnet Creek 32
Wareham 22
Warrenton 31
Warrington 22
Warsaw 52

Warwick 21
Washington 31
Washita 32
Waterloo 11
Wavre 11
Weert 49
Weihaiwei 38
Weimar 15
Wellington 34
Welshpool 21
Wenchow 38
Wendover 21
Weobley 22
Wesel 9
West Grinstead 21
Westbury 22
Wetzlar 16
Weymouth 22
Whitby 23
Whitchurch (Hants) 22
White Bird 32
Whitehaven 23
Whitehorse 29
Whitstable 23
Whydah 27
Wichita 32
Wichoo 38
Wigan 23
Wilsons Creek 31
Wilton 22
Wimborne 23
Winchelsea 22
Winchester 23
Windermere 23
Windhoek 26
Windward Is. 33
Winnipeg 29
Wisbech 21
Wismar 5
Wissembourg 17
Woking 23
Wolverhampton 23
Wonsan 38
Woodstock 22
Wootton Bassett 22
Worcester 23
Workington 23
Wörth 17
Wounded Knee 32
Wuchow 38
Wuhu 38
Württemberg 15
Würzburg 9

Xiengkhouang 58

Yalta 18
Yanaon 36
Yangyang 58
Yap 51
Yarmouth (I.O.W.) 22
Yarmouth (Norf.) 21
Yaroslavl 43
Yellowknife 29
Yenan 57
Yezd 47
Yochow 38
Yokohama 38
Yola 28
Yongdok 58
York 23
Ypres 42
Yukon 29

Zagreb 44
Zamboanga 50
Zanzibar 28
Zara 44
Zeeland 13
Zeerust 26
Zoutpansberg 26
Zug 13
Zürich 6